RESUMES
FOR
SCIENTIFIC
AND
TECHNICAL
CAREERS

VGM Professional Resumes Series

RESUMES FOR SCIENTIFIC AND TECHNICAL CAREERS

The Editors of
VGM Career Horizons

Printed on recyclable paper

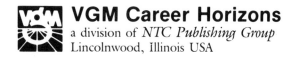

VGM Career Horizons
a division of *NTC Publishing Group*
Lincolnwood, Illinois USA

ACKNOWLEDGMENT

We would like to acknowledge the assistance of Martha K. Eberts in compiling and editing this book.

Library of Congress Cataloging-in-Publication Data

Resumes for scientific and technical careers/the editors of VGM Career Horizons.

    p. cm.— (VGM's professional resumes series)
    ISBN 0–8442-4157-1
    1. Scientists—Employment 2. Engineers—Employment. 3. Résumés
(Employment) I. VGM Career Horizons (Firm) II. Series.
Q147.R47 1993   93-13307
650'14–dc20   CIP

1995 Printing

Published by VGM Career Horizons, a division of NTC Publishing Group.
©1994 by NTC Publishing Group, 4255 West Touhy Avenue,
Lincolnwood (Chicago), Illinois 60646-1975, U.S.A.

4 5 6 7 8 9 0 VP 9 8 7 6 5 4 3 2

CONTENTS

Introduction

Your resume is your first impression on a prospective employer. Though you may be articulate, intelligent, and charming in person, a poor resume may prevent you from ever having the opportunity to demonstrate your interpersonal skills, because a poor resume may prevent you from ever being called for an interview. While few people have ever been hired solely on the basis of their resume, a well-written, well-organized resume can go a long way toward helping you land an interview. Your resume's main purpose is to get you that interview. The rest is up to you and the employer. If you both feel that you are right for the job and the job is right for you, chances are you will be hired.

A resume must catch the reader's attention yet still be easy to read and to the point. Resume styles have changed over the years. Today, brief and focused resumes are preferred. No longer do employers have the patience, or the time, to review several pages of solid type. A resume should be only one page long, if possible, and never more than two pages. Time is a precious commodity in today's business world and the resume that is concise and straightforward will usually be the one that gets noticed.

Let's not make the mistake, though, of assuming that writing a brief resume means that you can take less care in preparing it. A successful resume takes time and thought, and if you are willing to make the effort, the rewards are well worth it. Think of your resume as a sales tool with the product being you. You want to sell yourself to a prospective employer. This book is designed to help you prepare a resume that will help you further your career—to land that next job, or first job, or to return to the work force after years of absence. So, read on. Make the effort and reap the rewards that a strong resume can bring to your career. Let's get to it!

Chapter One

THE ELEMENTS OF A GOOD RESUME

A winning resume is made of the elements that employers are most interested in seeing when reviewing a job applicant. These basic elements are the essential ingredients of a successful resume and become the actual sections of your resume. The following is a list of elements that may be used in a resume. Some are essential; some are optional. We will be discussing these in this chapter in order to give you a better understanding of each element's role in the makeup of your resume:

1. Heading
2. Objective
3. Work Experience
4. Education
5. Honors
6. Activities
7. Certificates and Licenses
8. Professional Memberships
9. Special Skills
10. Personal Information
11. References

The first step in preparing your resume is to gather together information about yourself and your past accomplishments. Later you will refine this information, rewrite it in the most effective language, and organize it into the most attractive layout. First, let's take a look at each of these important elements individually.

Heading

The heading may seem to be a simple enough element in your resume, but be careful not to take it lightly. The heading should be placed at the top of your resume and should include your name, home address, and telephone numbers. If you can take calls at your current place of business, include your business number, since most employers will attempt to contact you during the business day. If this is not possible, or if you can afford it, purchase an answering machine that allows you to retrieve your messages while you are away from home. This way you can make sure you don't miss important phone calls. *Always* include your phone number on your resume. It is crucial that when prospective employers need to have immediate contact with you, they can.

Objective

When seeking a particular career path, it is important to list a job objective on your resume. This statement helps employers know the direction that you see yourself heading, so that they can determine whether your goals are in line with the position available. The objective is normally one sentence long and describes your employment goals clearly and concisely. See the sample resumes in this book for examples of objective statements.

The job objective will vary depending on the type of person you are, the field you are in, and the type of goals you have. It can be either specific or general, but it should always be to the point.

In some cases, this element is not necessary, but usually it is a good idea to include your objective. It gives your possible future employer an idea of where you are coming from and where you want to go.

The objective statement is better left out, however, if you are uncertain of the exact title of the job you seek. In such a case, the inclusion of an overly specific objective statement could result in your not being considered for a variety of acceptable positions; you should be sure to incorporate this information in your cover letter, instead.

Work Experience

This element is arguably the most important of them all. It will provide the central focus of your resume, so it is necessary that this section be as complete as possible. Only by examining your work experience in depth can you get to the heart of your accomplishments and present them in a way that demonstrates the strength of your qualifications. Of course, someone just out of school will have less work experience than someone who has been working for a number of years, but the amount of information isn't the most important thing—rather, how it is presented and how it highlights you as a person and as a worker will be what counts.

As you work on this section of your resume, be aware of the need for accuracy. You'll want to include all necessary information about each of your jobs, including job title, dates, employer, city, state, responsibilities, special projects, and accomplishments. Be sure to only list company accomplishments for which you were directly responsible. If you haven't participated in any special projects, that's all right—this area may not be relevant to certain jobs.

The most common way to list your work experience is in *reverse chronological order*. In other words, start with your most recent job and work your way backwards. This way your prospective employer sees your current (and often most important) job before seeing your past jobs. Your most recent position, if the most important, should also be the one that includes the most information, as compared to your previous positions. If you are just out of school, show your summer employment and part-time work, though in this case your education will most likely be more important than your work experience.

The following worksheets will help you gather information about your past jobs.

WORK EXPERIENCE
Job One:

Job Title _____

Dates _____

Employer _____

City, State _____

Major Duties _____

_____

_____

_____

_____

_____

_____

_____

Special Projects _____

_____

_____

_____

Accomplishments _____

_____

_____

_____

_____

_____

_____

_____

_____

Job Two:

Job Title _____

Dates _____

Employer _____

City, State _____

Major Duties _____

_____

_____

_____

_____

_____

_____

_____

Special Projects _____

_____

_____

_____

Accomplishments _____

_____

_____

_____

_____

_____

_____

_____

Job Three:

Job Title _____

Dates _____

Employer _____

City, State _____

Major Duties _____

_____

_____

_____

_____

_____

_____

Special Projects _____

_____

_____

_____

Accomplishments _____

_____

_____

_____

_____

_____

_____

_____

_____

Job Four:

Job Title _____

Dates _____

Employer _____

City, State _____

Major Duties _____

_____

_____

_____

_____

_____

_____

_____

Special Projects _____

_____

_____

_____

Accomplishments _____

_____

_____

_____

_____

_____

_____

_____

_____

Education

Education is the second most important element of a resume. Your educational background is often a deciding factor in an employer's decision to hire you. Be sure to stress your accomplishments in school with the same finesse that you stressed your accomplishments at work. If you are looking for your first job, your education will be your greatest asset, since your work experience will most likely be minimal. In this case, the education section becomes the most important. You will want to be sure to include any degrees or certificates you received, your major area of concentration, any honors, and any relevant activities. Again, be sure to list your most recent schooling first. If you have completed graduate-level work, begin with that and work in reverse chronological order through your undergraduate education. If you have completed an undergraduate degree, you may choose whether to list your high school experience or not. This should be done only if your high school grade-point average was well above average.

The following worksheets will help you gather information for this section of your resume. Also included are supplemental worksheets for honors and for activities. Sometimes honors and activities are listed in a section separate from education, most often near the end of the resume.

EDUCATION

School _____

Major or Area of Concentration _____

Degree _____

Date _____

School _____

Major or Area of Concentration _____

Degree _____

Date _____

Honors

Here, you should list any awards, honors, or memberships in honorary societies that you have received. Usually these are of an academic nature, but they can also be for special achievement in sports, clubs, or other school activities. Always be sure to include the name of the organization honoring you and the date(s) received. Use the worksheet below to help gather your honors information.

HONORS

Honor: _____

Awarding Organization: _____

Date(s): _____

Honor: _____

Awarding Organization: _____

Date(s): _____

Honor: _____

Awarding Organization: _____

Date(s): _____

Honor: _____

Awarding Organization: _____

Date(s): _____

Activities

You may have been active in different organizations or clubs during your years at school; often an employer will look at such involvement as evidence of initiative and dedication. Your ability to take an active role, and even a leadership role, in a group should be included on your resume. Use the worksheet provided to list your activities and accomplishments in this area. In general, you should exclude any organization the name of which indicates the race, creed, sex, age, marital status, color, or nation of origin of its members.

ACTIVITIES

Organization/Activity: _____

Accomplishments: _____

_____

_____

Organization/Activity: _____

Accomplishments: _____

_____

_____

Organization/Activity: _____

Accomplishments: _____

_____

_____

Organization/Activity: _____

Accomplishments: _____

_____

_____

As your work experience increases through the years, your school activities and honors will play less of a role in your resume, and eventually you will most likely only list your degree and any major honors you received. This is due to the fact that, as time goes by, your job performance becomes the most important element in your resume. Through time, your resume should change to reflect this.

Certificates and Licenses

The next potential element of your resume is certificates and licenses. You should list these if the job you are seeking requires them and you, of course, have acquired them. If you have applied for a license, but have not yet received it, use the phrase "application pending."

License requirements vary by state. If you have moved or you are planning to move to another state, be sure to check with the appropriate board or licensing agency in the state in which you are applying for work to be sure that you are aware of all licensing requirements.

Always be sure that all of the information you list is completely accurate. Locate copies of your licenses and certificates and check the exact date and name of the accrediting agency. Use the following worksheet to list your licenses and certificates.

CERTIFICATES AND LICENSES

Name of License: _____

Licensing Agency: _____

Date Issued: _____

Name of License: _____

Licensing Agency: _____

Date Issued: _____

Name of License: _____

Licensing Agency: _____

Date Issued: _____

Professional Memberships

Another potential element in your resume is a section listing professional memberships. Use this section to list involvement in professional associations, unions, and similar organizations. It is to your advantage to list any professional memberships that pertain to the job you are seeking. Be sure to include the dates of your involvement and whether you took part in any special activities or held any offices within the organization. Use the following worksheet to gather your information.

PROFESSIONAL MEMBERSHIPS

Name of Organization: _____

Offices Held: _____

Activities: _____

Date(s): _____

Name of Organization: _____

Offices Held: _____

Activities: _____

Date(s): _____

Name of Organization: _____

Offices Held: _____

Activities: _____

Date(s): _____

Name of Organization: _____

Offices Held: _____

Activities: _____

Date(s): _____

Special Skills

This section of your resume is set aside for mentioning any special abilities you have that could relate to the job you are seeking. This is the part of your resume where you have the opportunity to demonstrate certain talents and experiences that are not necessarily a part of your educational or work experience. Common examples include fluency in a foreign language, or knowledge of a particular computer application.

Special skills can encompass a wide range of your talents—remember to be sure that whatever skills you list relate to the type of work you are looking for.

Personal Information

Some people include "Personal" information on their resumes. This is not generally recommended, but you might wish to include it if you think that something in your personal life, such as a hobby or talent, has some bearing on the position you are seeking. This type of information is often referred to at the beginning of an interview, when it is used as an "ice breaker." Of course, personal information regarding age, marital status, race, religion, or sexual preference should never appear on any resume.

References

References are not usually listed on the resume, but a prospective employer needs to know that you have references who may be contacted if necessary. All that is necessary to include in your resume regarding references is a sentence at the bottom stating, "References are available upon request." If a prospective employer requests a list of references, be sure to have one ready. Also, check with whomever you list to see if it is all right for you to use them as a reference. Forewarn them that they may receive a call regarding a reference for you. This way they can be prepared to give you the best reference possible.

Chapter Two

WRITING YOUR RESUME

*N*ow that you have gathered together all of the information for each of the sections of your resume, it's time to write out each section in a way that will get the attention of whoever is reviewing it. The type of language you use in your resume will affect its success. You want to take the information you have gathered and translate it into a language that will cause a potential employer to sit up and take notice.

Resume writing is not like expository writing or creative writing. It embodies a functional, direct writing style and focuses on the use of action words. By using action words in your writing, you more effectively stress past accomplishments. Action words help demonstrate your initiative and highlight your talents. Always use verbs that show strength and reflect the qualities of a "doer." By using action words, you characterize yourself as a person who takes action, and this will impress potential employers.

The following is a list of verbs commonly used in resume writing. Use this list to choose the action words that can help your resume become a strong one:

administered	introduced
advised	invented
analyzed	maintained
arranged	managed
assembled	met with
assumed responsibility	motivated
billed	negotiated
built	operated
carried out	orchestrated
channeled	ordered
collected	organized
communicated	oversaw
compiled	performed
completed	planned
conducted	prepared
contacted	presented
contracted	produced
coordinated	programmed
counseled	published
created	purchased
cut	recommended
designed	recorded
determined	reduced
developed	referred
directed	represented
dispatched	researched
distributed	reviewed
documented	saved
edited	screened
established	served as
expanded	served on
functioned as	sold
gathered	suggested
handled	supervised
hired	taught
implemented	tested
improved	trained
inspected	typed
interviewed	wrote

Now take a look at the information you put down on the work experience worksheets. Take that information and rewrite it in paragraph form, using verbs to highlight your actions and accomplishments. Let's look at an example, remembering that what matters here is the writing style, and not the particular job responsibilities given in our sample.

WORK EXPERIENCE
Regional Sales Manager

Manager of sales representatives from seven states. Responsible for twelve food chain accounts in the East. In charge of directing the sales force in planned selling toward specific goals. Supervisor and trainer of new sales representatives. Consulting for customers in the areas of inventory management and quality control.

Special Projects: Coordinator and sponsor of annual food industry sales seminar.

Accomplishments: Monthly regional volume went up 25 percent during my tenure while, at the same time, a proper sales/cost ratio was maintained. Customer/company relations improved significantly.

Below is the rewritten version of this information, using action words. Notice how much stronger it sounds.

WORK EXPERIENCE
Regional Sales Manager

Managed sales representatives from seven states. Handled twelve food chain accounts in the eastern United States. Directed the sales force in planned selling towards specific goals. Supervised and trained new sales representatives. Consulted for customers in the areas of inventory management and quality control. Coordinated and sponsored the annual Food Industry Seminar. Increased monthly regional volume 25 percent and helped to improve customer/company relations during my tenure.

Another way of constructing the work experience section is by using actual job descriptions. Job descriptions are rarely written using the proper resume language, but they do include all the information necessary to create this section of your resume. Take the description of one of the jobs your are including on your resume (if you have access to it), and turn it into an action-oriented paragraph. Below is an example of a job description followed by a version of the same description written using action words. Again, pay attention to the style of writing, as the details of your own work experience will be unique.

PUBLIC ADMINISTRATOR I

Responsibilities: Coordinate and direct public services to meet the needs of the nation, state, or community. Analyze problems; work with special committees and public agencies; recommend solutions to governing bodies.

Aptitudes and Skills: Ability to relate to and communicate with people; solve complex problems through analysis; plan, organize, and implement policies and programs. Knowledge of political systems; financial management; personnel administration; program evaluation; organizational theory.

WORK EXPERIENCE
Public Administrator I

Wrote pamphlets and conducted discussion groups to inform citizens of legislative processes and consumer issues. Organized and supervised 25 interviewers. Trained interviewers in effective communication skills.

Now that you have learned how to word your resume, you are ready for the next step in your quest for a winning resume: assembly and layout.

Chapter Three

ASSEMBLY AND LAYOUT

*A*t this point, you've gathered all the necessary information for your resume, and you've rewritten it using the language necessary to impress potential employers. Your next step is to assemble these elements in a logical order and then to lay them out on the page neatly and attractively in order to achieve the desired effect: getting that interview.

Assembly

The order of the elements in a resume makes a difference in its overall effect. Obviously, you would not want to put your name and address in the middle of the resume or your special skills section at the top. You want to put the elements in an order that stresses your most important achievements, not the less pertinent information. For example, if you recently graduated from school and have no full-time work experience, you will want to list your education before you list any part-time jobs you may have held during school. On the other hand, if you have been gainfully employed for several years and currently hold an important position in your company, you will want to list your work experience ahead of your education, which has become less pertinent with time.

There are some elements that are always included in your resume and some that are optional. Following is a list of essential and optional elements:

Essential	*Optional*
Name	Job Objective
Address	Honors
Phone Number	Special Skills
Work Experience	Professional Memberships
Education	Activities
References Phrase	Certificates and Licenses
	Personal Information

Your choice of optional sections depends on your own background and employment needs. Always use information that will put you and your abilities in a favorable light. If your honors are impressive, then be sure to include them in your resume. If your activities in school demonstrate particular talents necessary for the job you are seeking, then allow space for a section on activities. Each resume is unique, just as each person is unique.

Types of Resumes

So far, our discussion about resumes has involved the most common type—the *reverse chronological* resume, in which your most recent job is listed first and so on. This is the type of resume usually preferred by human resources directors, and it is the one most frequently used. However, in some cases this style of presentation is not the most effective way to highlight your skills and accomplishments.

For someone reentering the work force after many years or someone looking to change career fields, the *functional resume* may work best. This type of resume focuses more on achievement and less on the sequence of your work history. In the functional resume, your experience is presented by what you have accomplished and the skills you have developed in your past work.

A functional resume can be assembled from the same information you collected for your chronological resume. The main difference lies in how you organize this information. Essentially, the work experience section becomes two sections, with your job duties and accomplishments comprising one section and your employer's name, city, state, your position, and the dates employed making up another section. The first section is placed near the top of the resume, just below the job objective section, and can be called *Accomplishments* or *Achievements*. The second section, containing the bare essentials of your employment history, should come after the accomplishments section and can be titled *Work Experience* or *Employment History*. The other sections of your resume remain the same. The work experience section is the only one affected in the functional resume. By placing the section that focuses on your achievements first, you thereby draw attention to these achievements. This puts less emphasis on who you worked for and more emphasis on what you did and what you are capable of doing.

For someone changing careers, emphasis on skills and achievements is essential. The identities of previous employers, which may be unrelated to one's new job field, need to be downplayed. The functional resume accomplishes this task. For someone reentering the work force after many years, a functional resume is the obvious choice. If you lack full-time work experience, you will need to draw attention away from this fact and instead focus on your skills and abilities gained possibly through volunteer activities or part-time work. Education may also play a more important role in this resume.

Which type of resume is right for you will depend on your own personal circumstances. It may be helpful to create a chronological *and* a functional resume and then compare the two to find out which is more suitable. The sample resumes found in this book include both chronological and functional resumes. Use these resumes as guides to help you decide on the content and appearance of your own resume.

Layout

Once you have decided which elements to include in your resume and you have arranged them in an order that makes sense and emphasizes your achievements and abilities, then it is time to work on the physical layout of your resume.

There is no single appropriate layout that applies to every resume, but there are a few basic rules to follow in putting your resume on paper:

1. Leave a comfortable margin on the sides, top, and bottom of the page (usually 1 to 1½ inches).

2. Use appropriate spacing between the sections (usually 2 to 3 line spaces are adequate).

3. Be consistent in the *type* of headings you use for the different sections of your resume. For example, if you capitalize the heading EMPLOYMENT HISTORY, don't use initial capitals and underlining for a heading of equal importance, such as Education.

4. Always try to fit your resume onto one page. If you are having trouble fitting all your information onto one page, perhaps you are trying to say too much. Try to edit out any repetitive or unnecessary information or possibly shorten descriptions of earlier jobs. Be ruthless. Maybe you've included too many optional sections.

CHRONOLOGICAL RESUME

Michael G. Block   Home: (617) 555-4813
75 Eldridge Court   Work: (617) 555-6741
Cambridge, MA 02138

OBJECTIVE: To utilize my communication, problem-solving, and decision-making skills in a professional position which offers development and increasing levels of responsibility.

EDUCATION: Ivy Technical Institute - Associate Degree
               Material Requirements Planning Seminars - Certificate
               ITT Technical Institute - Certificate

EXPERIENCE:

10/89 - Present   Lincoln Engineering - Cambridge, MA
                   Service Technician Assistant - Assist service technicians in installing heating and air conditioning units in various city-wide industrial and residential applications. Provide pick-up and delivery service. Operate hydraulic forklift. Use acetylene/oxygen cutting torch and other related trade tools.

4/84 - 9/89   Taylor Components Group - Concord, NH
                   Programmer Technician - Developed and maintained applications for various departments. Created screen formats for program access using FOCUS Report Writer language.

                   Trainer - Provided end users with working understanding of computer. Taught in-house seminar on creating Bills-of-Material using Cullinet on-line software package.

                   Help Service - Allocated, created, and deleted data sets for end users. Provided troubleshooting assistance. Served as liaison between Management Information Service and various departments.

                   Documentation - Prepared and provided end users with step-by-step procedures for using computer. Prepared user manual for Bills-of-Materials seminar.

4/79 - 3/84   Taylor Components Group - Concord, NH
                   Draftsman - Prepared detailed drawings of parts from layouts and sketches using standard drawings and drafting and measuring tools and instruments.

FUNCTIONAL RESUME

MICHAEL COLLINS
**381 East 81st, #27
New York, NY 10028
(212) 555-3953**

Award winning Technical Educator and Computer Support Specialist which can make me an outstanding contributor to your organization in the areas of:

MANAGEMENT INFORMATION SYSTEMS
TECHNICAL EDUCATION
COMPUTER SYSTEMS SUPPORT

EDUCATION

**U.S. NAVY ELECTRONIC TRAINING
1979-1982**

**SUBMARINER CERTIFICATION
1980**

TRAINING AND EXPERTISE

Super Computer Integrated Systems
Mainframes through Micros
Peripheral Equipment
Personal Computer Applications

PERSONAL

Football referee in Collegiate League
Music - piano and trumpet

you've included too many optional sections. Don't let the idea of having to tell every detail about your life get in the way of producing a resume that is simple and straightforward. The more compact your resume, the easier it will be to read and the better impression it will make for you.

Try experimenting with various layouts until you find one that looks good to you. It may be a good idea to show your final layout to people who can tell you what they think is right or wrong with it. Ask them what impresses them most about your resume. Make sure that is what you want most to emphasize. If it isn't, you may want to consider making changes in your layout until the necessary information is emphasized. Use the sample resumes in chapter 5 to get some ideas for laying out your resume.

Putting Your Resume in Print

Your resume should be typed or printed on good quality $8^{1}/_{2}'' \times 11''$ bond paper. You want to make as good an impression as possible with your resume; therefore, quality paper is a necessity. If you have access to a word processor with a good printer, make use of it. If not, a typewriter that produces good, clean copy should be just fine.

After you have produced a clean original, you will want to go ahead and make duplicate copies of it. Usually a copy shop is your best bet for producing copies without smudges or streaks. Make sure you have the copy shop use quality bond paper for all copies of your resume. Ask for a sample copy before they run your entire order. After copies are made, check each copy for cleanliness and clarity.

Another more costly option is to have your resume typeset and printed by a printer. This will provide the most attractive resume, but most likely the neat, clean, hand-typed resume will have the same effect as the typeset resume at far less expense.

Proofreading

After you have finished typing the master copy of your resume and before you go to have it copied or printed, you must thoroughly check it for typing and spelling errors. Have several people read it over just in case you may have missed an error. Misspelled words and typing mistakes will not make a good impression on a prospective employer. They are a bad reflection on your writing ability and your attention to detail. With thorough and conscientious proofreading, these mistakes can be avoided. The following are some rules of capitalization and punctuation that may come in handy when proofreading your resume:

Rules of Capitalization

- Capitalize proper nouns, such as names of schools, colleges and universities, names of companies, and brand names of products.
- Capitalize major words in the names and titles of books, tests, and articles that appear in the body of your resume.
- Capitalize words in major section headings of your resume.
- Do not capitalize words just because they seem important.
- When in doubt, consult a manual of style such as *Words Into Type* (Prentice-Hall); or *The Chicago Manual of Style*, (The University of Chicago Press). Your local library can help you locate these and others.

Rules of Punctuation

- Use a comma to separate words in a series.
- Use a semicolon to separate series of words that already include commas within the series.
- Use a semicolon to separate independent clauses that are not joined by a conjunction.
- Use a period to end a sentence.
- Use a colon to show that the examples or details that follow expand or amplify the preceding phrase.
- Avoid the use of dashes.
- Avoid the use of brackets.
- If you use any punctuation in an unusual way in your resume, be consistent in its use.
- Whenever you are uncertain, consult a style manual.

Chapter Four

THE COVER LETTER

*O*nce your resume has been assembled, laid out, and printed to your satisfaction, the next and final step before distribution is to write your cover letter. Though there may be instances where you deliver your resume in person, most often you will be sending it through the mail. Resumes sent through the mail always need an accompanying letter that briefly introduces you and your resume. The purpose of the cover letter is to get a potential employer to read your resume, just as the purpose of your resume is to get that same potential employer to call you for an interview.

Like your resume, your cover letter should be clean, neat, and direct. A cover letter usually includes the following information:

1. Your name and address.

2. The date.

3. The name and address of the person and company to whom you are sending your resume.

4. The salutation ("Dear Mr." or "Dear Ms." followed by the person's last name, or "To Whom It May Concern").

5. An opening paragraph explaining why you are writing (in response to an ad, the result of a previous meeting, at the suggestion of someone you both know) and indicating your interest in the job being offered.

6. One or two more paragraphs that tell why you want to work for the company and what qualifications and experience you can bring to that company.

7. A final paragraph that closes the letter and requests that you be contacted for an interview. You may mention here that your references are available upon request.

8. The closing ("Sincerely," or "Yours Truly," followed by your signature with your name typed under it).

Your cover letter, including all of the information above, should be no more than one page in length. The language used should be polite, businesslike, and to the point. Do not attempt to tell your life story in the cover letter. A long and cluttered letter will only serve to put off the reader. Remember, you only need to mention a few of your accomplishments and skills in the cover letter. The rest of your information is in your resume. Each and every achievement should not be mentioned twice. If your cover letter is a success, your resume will be read and all pertinent information reviewed by your prospective employer.

Producing the Cover Letter

Cover letters should always be typed individually, since they are always written to particular individuals and companies. Never use a form letter for your cover letter. Each one should be as personal as possible. Of course, once you have written and rewritten your first cover letter to the point where you are satisfied with it, you certainly can use similar wording in subsequent letters.

After you have typed your cover letter on quality bond paper, be sure to proofread it as thoroughly as you did your resume. Again, spelling errors are a sure sign of carelessness, and you don't want that to be a part of your first impression on a prospective employer. Make sure to handle the letter and resume carefully to avoid any smudges, and then mail both your cover letter and resume in an appropriate sized envelope. Be sure to keep an accurate record of all the resumes you send out and the results of each mailing.

Numerous sample cover letters appear at the end of the book. Use them as models for your own cover letter or to get an idea of how cover letters are put together. Remember, every one is unique and depends on the particular circumstances of the individual writing it and the job for which he or she is applying.

About a week after mailing resumes and cover letters to potential employers, you will want to contact them by telephone. Confirm that your resume arrived, and ask whether an interview might be possible. Getting your foot in the door during this call is half the battle of a job search, and a strong resume and cover letter will help you immeasurably.

Chapter Five

SAMPLE RESUMES

This chapter contains dozens of sample resumes for people pursuing a wide variety of jobs and careers within this field.

There are many different styles of resumes in terms of graphic layout and presentation of information. These samples also represent people with varying amounts of education and work experience. Use these samples to model your own resume after. Choose one resume, or borrow elements from several different resumes to help you construct your own.

Jason Alexander
345 East 82nd Street
New York, NY 10028

Office: (212) 555-3654   **Home: (212) 555-9065**

OBJECTIVE	Senior MIS management position in an international firm with long-range personal growth potential.
SUMMARY	Fifteen years MIS experience in developing large-scale commercial business systems. Solid technical background in multi-language programming and system design with extensive user interfacing. Last ten years held increasingly important MIS management positions.
EDUCATION	Cornell University, B.S., Mathematics (1964), M.A., Statistics (1968).
TECHNICAL	Equipment: IBM 370/43XX/30XX, DOS/VSE, OS/MVS, CICS, TSO/ROSCOE, SPERRY 1100/71/91, DMS/TIP. Languages: BASIC, COBOL, FORTRAN, INQUIRE, MARK IV, RPG, SMP.

EXPERIENCE

1983-Present   **DELOITTE & TOUCHE, NEW YORK, NEW YORK**
Assistant MIS Director, Systems & Programming (1985-Present)

Direct a systems and programming organization of 40 MIS professionals in the development and enhancement of the firm's internal business system. Overseeing major developments in the areas of client management, general ledger, accounts receivable, personnel, and partnership accounting.

Manager, MIS Applications Development (1983-1985)

Staffed and directed a Systems & Programming group of 20 MIS professionals in the design and development of a firm-wide on-line database to maintain the firm's client base and to track the professional consulting staff's time and expenses.

- Directed project definition and functional analysis phase of project life-cycle.

- Recruited 10 full-time analysts and programmers to develop detailed systems design and specifications using top-down structured methodology.

- Coordinated the design and development of a complex database structure to support the on-line informational needs of the firm.

- Initiated the development of naming standards, program skeletons, reusable code, and macro routines to assist and standardize the program construction phase of development.

- Developed and instituted a basecase testing methodology for the comprehensive testing and quality assurance of the developed system.

1973-1983　　　**IBM CORPORATION, WHITE PLAINS, NEW YORK**
Manager, MIS Development Projects (1981-1983)

Coordinated migration and implementation of financial and administrative systems being developed by European operations for use in the Latin American affiliates.

- Defined and implemented migration strategy and procedure for all MIS activities including software, testing, and affiliate training.

- Conceived, designed, and negotiated first time maintenance and emergency procedures for ongoing production support between European development center and Latin American affiliates.

- Initiated, developed, and implemented on-line strategy on optimum cost effective general guidelines and procedures for all CICS applications in Latin America.

Manager, System Projects (1976-1981)

Developed and managed increasingly complex systems culminating in the direction of 2-year retail finance and leasing system.

- Directed and implemented front-end CICS system that reduced input from 10 to 3 days.

- Expanded and revamped existing system to mechanize all edits/validations and provide timely management reporting.

Directed systems and programming staff of 8 in development/maintenance of systems in areas of supply/service billing, equipment control, collection services, insurance loss, and vehicle asset tracking.

- Conceived, directed, and implemented modularized table system.

- Instituted "Block" system releases resulting in greater throughput of user requests and reduced direct overhead costs.

Senior Programming Consultant (1973-1976)

Project leader of 5 systems and programming personnel in maintenance and enhancement of monthly equipment billing system.

Organized MARK IV Coordinator function to support end users of marketing, finance, and service/distribution in developing their own inquiries for management information. Designed and programmed MARK IV applications.

PABLO SANCHEZ
500 Briar Patch Road
Frankfort, KY 40601
(502) 555-8750

OBJECTIVE

Foreman or Heavy Equipment Operator.

PROFESSIONAL EXPERIENCE

From June 1990 to Present

Scraper Superintendent, Kentucky Department of Transportation.
- Involved in extensive training program initiated by state to give hands on training to operators and mechanical staff on Cat models 631E, D10N, 16G.
- Trained operators in the loading sequence by utilizing the Chain Loading method.
- Supervised and directed scraper fleet on a daily basis.
- Supervised and operated dozer on earth fill dam project.
- Operated truck fleet on overburden removal in a gold mine.

From July 1985 to January 1990

Owner and Operator of trucking/construction company, Sanchez Construction.
- Worked on small to medium sized construction projects for private sector as well as Soil Conservation Service and U.S. Army Corps of Engineers.
- Assistant Quality Control official for Soil Conservation Service and U.S. Army Corps of Engineers on flood clean up.
- Instituted my own maintenance program also did most of mechanical work.
- Trucking for such contractors as Mason Corp., Daniel Industries, SJ Almaden, PB Snyder, Kentucky Excavating, Anton Construction, Hugh Bowman Contracting, and Landfill Crossroad Inc.

EQUIPMENT SKILLS

From 1981 to 1985

Caterpillar:	Dozers, Loaders, Scrapers, Excavators
Komatsu:	Dozers, Excavators
Clark:	Excavators
John Deere:	Excavators
Holland:	Belt Loaders

EDUCATION

Mason County Joint Vocational School
Diesel Mechanics and Welding
Graduated 1980

PERSONAL

Organizations	Fraternal Order of Elks
	Fraternal Order of Police Lodge #55
	International Union of Operating Engineers
	Local #555, Frankfort, KY
Hobbies	Hunting, Fishing, Skiing

REFERENCES

Available upon request.

MARK F. FULTON

Current Address:
78 Prairie Road
Columbus, OH 43216
(614) 555-3981

Permanent Address:
26 Fernwood Road
Steubenville, OH 40605
(614) 555-1807

OBJECTIVE   To obtain a position in construction engineering and management.

EDUCATION   **Ohio State University**, Columbus, OH
Master of Science, Civil Engineering
Graduated May 1993

University of Dayton, Dayton, OH
Bachelor of Engineering, Civil Engineering
Graduated Cum Laude, May 1992

HONORS   Regents Fellowship, Ohio State University
Harry Long Memorial Prize, University of Dayton
Dean's List for six semesters, University of Dayton

EXPERIENCE
SUMMER 91   **Ohio Department of Transportation** Steubenville, OH
Engineer in Training 1
Worked with Resident Engineer's office. Responsible for inspecting the construction of a reinforced concrete bridge and roadway. Made daily reports and kept detailed records of contractor performance and progress.

SUMMER 90   **Hayes, Jones, and Bowers** Steubenville, OH
Engineering Aide
Worked with professional engineers in the design of roadways and structures. Responsible for hydrologic aspects of highway design. Participated on in-depth bridge inspection.

SUMMER 89   **Hayes, Jones, and Bowers** Steubenville, OH
Engineering Aide
Worked with professional engineers in design of wastewater treatment plants and sewer systems. Responsible for AutoCAD drawings and checking design calculations.

**ADDITIONAL
INFORMATION**   Passed the April 1993 Engineer in Training exam.

REFERENCES   Prof. B. William Gebbs, Ohio State University, 80 Lawrence .Hall, Columbus, OH 43210

Prof. Roger K. Hadley, University of Dayton, P.O. Box 8020-C, Dayton, OH 45469

PATRICIA BUTTERFIELD
1480 Dean Road
Sacramento, CA 95819
(916) 555-9306

OBJECTIVE: Desire a challenging and rewarding position in the environmental field.

EDUCATION: Bachelor of Science, University of California at San Diego, 1982. Major in Aquatic Biology, Minor in Natural Resources.

EXPERIENCE: CALIFORNIA DEPARTMENT OF ENVIRONMENTAL MANAGEMENT, Sacramento, CA.

March 1989 to
Present

Environmental Project Manager, State Cleanup Section, Environmental Response.
- Managed the cleanup of hazardous waste sites.
- Contracted the disposal of hazardous materials.
- Negotiated cleanup issues with PRPs.
- Conducted field sampling and contractor overview.

July 1988 to
March 1989

Environmental Manager, Facilities Planning Section, Water Management.
- Implemented outreach program for building of treatment facilities in small communities.
- Performed primary and secondary review of facilities planning documents for the construction grants program.
- Interfaced with engineering firms and evaluated project costs.

April 1984 to
July 1988

Environmental Scientist, Permits Section, Water Management.
- Reviewed program documents and managed implementation of municipal programs.
- Aided in the implementation of the state pretreatment program.
- Wrote permits for industrial users, NPDES, and land application.
- Conducted audits of municipal pretreatment programs and inspected manufacturing facilities.

LAKE SHASTA RECREATION AREA, Shasta, CA.

April 1983 to
Sept. 1983

Park Naturalist.
- Managed the activities of park nature center.
- Conducted environmental programs for park visitors.

AFFILIATIONS: Institute of Hazardous Materials Management
National Wildlife Federation
Water Pollution Control Federation

Guy Fortune

Present Address
450 West Pontiac Lane
East Lansing, MI 48824
(517) 555-6534

Permanent Address
1929 Ford Drive
Detroit, MI 48183
(313) 555-4631

Objective   Obtain engineering employment involving design and construction of roads, bridges, and associated structures.

Experience   Senior Class Project: Design of Concrete Slab Road Test Facility. Spring 1993.

Appleby Inc., Detroit, MI
Skilled Laborer/Foreman: Site surveys and layouts, excavation, concrete placement and finishing, plumbing, carpentry, and equipment operator. Summers 1990-1992.

Lowell Construction, Detroit, MI
General Laborer: Concrete placement and finishing, carpentry, and excavation. Summer 1987.

Parr Marketing Co., Detroit, MI
Sales Representative. 12/90-1/91.

L.D. Jones & Sons, East Lansing, MI
Retail Lumber Yard Helper. 6/88-12/88.

Prairie Cycles, East Lansing, MI
Bicycle Repair Technician. 10/87-12/87.

Education   Michigan State University, 5/93.
B.S. in Civil Engineering.
Dean's List, 1990-1991.

University of Michigan, 5/88.
Major - Electrical Engineering.
Dean's List, 1988.

Registration   Certified Engineer in Training, June 19, 1993

Affiliations   American Society of Civil Engineers

Interests   Concrete Canoe Competition, Automotive Repair, Active Sports

JOHN K. LAI
20 West Concord Street
Dover, NH 03820
(603) 555-1703

EDUCATION: B.S., Civil Engineering, University of New Hampshire

CAREER SUMMARY:
Extensive experience in program management on complex construction projects. Managed all phases of project administration, contract development, and claims negotiation. Proven knowledge and skills to interact with professionals, contractors, and labor personnel.

EXPERIENCE:
1991 - MAY 1993   -   Johnson, Inc.
Position: Resident Engineer, North Shore Interceptor, Phase IV.
Location: Concord, New Hampshire
Duties: Supervise performance of construction contractors. Project included tunnels, deep shafts, chambers, odor control structures, and appurtenant facilities.

1990 - 1991   -   Bechtel
Position: Project Manager
Location: Hanford, Washington
Duties: Special consultant to the Department of Energy and Rockwell International for design and construction of underground and shafts facilities for storage of nuclear waste.

1988 - 1990   -   Bechtel
Position: Project Manager Construction Services
Location: Los Angeles, California
Duties: Prepared division budgets, long-range plans, and project proposals. Assigned construction personnel to projects. Area Construction Manager on the proposal for Los Angeles Subway Construction. Supervised preparation of procedures for construction of power generation plant and coal mine in China.

REGISTRATION: Professional Engineer, New Hampshire

ASSOCIATIONS: American Management Association
                   Society of American Military Engineers
                   Society of Mining Engineers

NAME: Michael S. Flowers

ADDRESS: 4459 Palm Drive
Las Vegas, NV 89154

PHONE: (702) 555 - 8666

EDUCATION:

1957-1958	University of Nevada, Reno, NV, Business Administration Major
1959-1960	Truckee Meadows Community College, Truckee, NV, Math Major
1960-1965	International Correspondence School, Civil Engineering Certificate
1983-1985	University of Southern California, Los Angeles, CA, Master of Business Administration

EXPERIENCE:

DESERT CONSTRUCTION, INC., Las Vegas, NV

9/90 - Present   **MANAGER OF ESTIMATING AND ENGINEERING** - Oversee and manage all estimating and engineering.

L.A. SMITH CONSTRUCTION CO., San Diego, CA

4/87 - 9/90   **MANAGER OF ESTIMATING AND ENGINEERING** - Heavy/Marine Division. Supervise division engineer and estimating manager for heavy and marine estimating and construction. Market segments are heavy engineering, northeast transit, and hazardous waste work.

BROWNELL CORPORATION, Long Beach, CA

11/81 - 3/87   **VICE-PRESIDENT/MANAGER HEAVY ESTIMATING** - Established joint venture procedures. Arranged complete estimates for joint ventures. Supervised estimators in estimating and bidding projects such as: treatment plants, power plants, airport terminals, piers and docks, pumping plants, subways, and mass transit. Upgraded computer format for heavy estimating.

FLOWERS CONSULTING, Los Angeles, CA

5/80 - 11/81   **PRESIDENT** - Formed company to provide consulting services. Advised Southern California Water District in reconstructing a CPM schedule of a water treatment plant.

KAREN S. ADAMS
1685 MOUNTAIN DRIVE
TUCSON, AZ 85720
(602) 555-8960

CAREER OBJECTIVE

Project management for medium-sized firm. Working toward international construction management with an eye on environmental compatibility.

PERSONAL DATA

Active, sports-oriented, enjoy reading, travel, people, and languages. Extensive music, dance, and theater training.

PROFESSIONAL EXPERIENCE

1989 -
Present
UA Physical Plant, Tucson, AZ
Position: Project Coordinator
Responsibilities include:
- Start to finish management of construction projects.
- Estimating, assembling technical teams, surveying and layout, some design/drafting/ACAD, specs, job supervision, and inspection.
- Re-design of local "problem" intersection.

Prior to
1989
Thirteen years in the construction industry, starting as a laborer in 1973, ending as a journeyman, formsetter, and concrete finisher. Experience as crew foreman, tractor operator, job supervisor, and estimator. Other experience includes many other construction includes, motorcycle mechanic, waitress, and own custom woodworking shop.

STRENGTHS AND CAPABILITIES

- Detail and big picture-oriented.
- Anticipating and solving problems.
- Very good with numbers in the field and with people.
- Bring projects in on time and within budget without sacrificing quality.

ACADEMIC BACKGROUND

1989-1993
Senior in Civil Engineering at the University of Arizona, Tucson, AZ. G.P.A. 3.85, Outstanding Junior and Outstanding Service Awards for 1990. Honors recipient the past 3 years. Stressing construction management, environmental and geotechnical engineering, IBM and Mac computer literacy, and French. Graduated May 1993.

REFERENCES

Available upon request.

Josh C. Curtain

655 Kelton Avenue, Detroit, MI 48125 (313) 555-7300

OBJECTIVE
A position that will utilize my academic background and experience in outside industrial sales.

EDUCATIONAL BACKGROUND

1980 - 1984
University of Windsor, Windsor, Ontario. Bachelor of Commerce. Concentrating in marketing, finance, and accounting.

PROFESSIONAL EXPERIENCE
April 1986 to present: Sales Engineer/Outside Sales Representative, Washington Electric, Detroit, MI. Responsible for outside sales of special machinery and project coordinator in the Southeastern Michigan, Ohio, and Ontario areas. Launch and follow progress of machines from design to testing. Act as liaison between client/customer and plant. Assist in pricing and custom design of all machines. Develop and design brochures as selling tool. Continuously search for new and innovative techniques to reach the company's specific market. Deal predominantly with the auto, food, heating and cooling industries.

SPECIAL SKILLS
Working knowledge of WordPerfect, Wordstar, and Lotus 1-2-3. Capable of making cold calls.
Very familiar with Detroit automotive market and related industries.

REFERENCES
Available upon request.

Vajid L. Singh
P.O. Box 1296
Stanford, CA 94309
(415) 555-0701

EDUCATION

<u>Master of Business Administration, June 1993</u>
Stanford University, Stanford, CA

<u>Bachelor of Technology, Civil Engineering, July 1987</u>
Institute of Technology, New Delhi, India

EMPLOYMENT

August 1987 –
July 1991

<u>Field Engineer</u>
Nardini Co. Ltd. (subsidiary of Ferguson Construction plc, United Kingdom)
New Delhi, India

- Managed construction sites as independent profit centers consistently achieving target margins.
- Supervised and directed work of 4 foreman and 25 skilled workers.
- Prepared cost estimates and quantity surveys for contract bids and analyzed project proposals.
- Collected, analyzed, and interpreted data pertaining to financial and production performance of site as well as wrote reports to facilitate control.
- Negotiated and liaisoned on a regular basis with labor unions and clients.

Sept. 1991 –
June 1993

<u>Graduate Teaching Assistant</u>
Stanford University
Stanford, CA

- Graded, tutored, and advised students enrolled in Operations Management class.

Sept. 1991 –
June 1993

<u>Microcomputer Laboratory Monitor</u>
Stanford University
Stanford, CA

- Guided and assisted students and faculty in the productive use of analytical, graphics, and wordprocessing PC software.
- Served over 100 users during peak laboratory usage.

COMPUTER BACKGROUND

Proficient in use of following PC programs, operating systems, and languages: RBase for DOS, Statgraphics, SPSS-PC+, Lotus 1-2-3, Quattro Pro, Excel, Harvard Graphics, MS-DOS, Netware, Pascal, BASIC, FORTRAN.

AWARDS & HONORS

Awarded $5,000 fellowship in 1987 by Education Trust to pursue study in the U.S.
Member – Beta Gamma Sigma (national honor society for business students)

REFERENCES

Supplied on request.

KENNETH H. CROTHERS

80 Cavendish Drive   (608) 555-9783
Madison, WI 53714   (608) 555-6034

EDUCATION

Bachelor of Arts of Architecture, December 1992
University of Wisconsin, Madison, WI

EXPERIENCE

Landscape Architect   **April 1993 - Present**
NANCY'S NURSERIES & GARDEN CENTER, INC., Madison, WI
- Conduct cost estimates.
- Develop designs for residential/commercial landscapes.
- Lead final design presentation for client.

Partner/Designer   **January 1993 - April 1993**
SELF-EMPLOYED HOME RENOVATOR, Milwaukee, WI
- Developed ideas for home interior renovations.
- Implemented ideas/designs according to local building codes.

Assistant Layout Supervisor   **May 1992 - September 1992**
BRADFORD MALLS, Milwaukee, WI
- Assisted in the planning and layout operation for new and existing mall and restaurant parking areas.

Site Surveyor   **May 1991 - August 1991**
K&R INSTALLATIONS, Milwaukee, WI
- Installed recreational decks.

MILITARY

United States Marine Corps.   Rank: Lance Corporal
September 1987 - April 1991
Anti-Armor Team Leader and Explosives Expert

RELATED SKILLS

- Operate CAD system
- Read wide variety of design prints

PERSONAL DATA

- Willing to travel/relocate
- Hobbies: hockey, baseball, golf, white water rafting

REFERENCES

Available upon request.

WILLIAM LYON COOPER
4142 Telegraph Avenue, #9
Berkeley, CA 94709
(408) 555-7756

Work History

1989-present   **Environmental Systems Group**, Oakland, CA
Project Manager. Prepare environmental assessments, facilities plans, and specialized reports. Collect data through research and field surveys. Conceptual design of wastewater treatment plants, water treatment plants, collection/distribution systems, etc.

1985-1989   **Oregon State University Bookstore**, Corvallis, OR
Began as cashier, advanced to clerk--special order; further advancement to assistant branch manager. Ordered stock and inventory supplies; cleared and balanced daily sales; supervised hourly employees and customer relations. Worked 40 hours a week while attending college for three years.

Education

1984-1988   **Oregon State University**, Corvallis, OR
Bachelor of Science in Public Affairs, majors in Environmental Science and Environmental Affairs. Requirements completed December 1988. Concentration grade point average 2.9. Courses included Biology, Chemistry, Energy and the Environment, Environmental Techniques, Geology, Hydrogeology, Lake and Watershed Management, Law and Public Policy, Physics, and Urban Development.

Interests

Fishing, hunting, hiking, boating, and football.
Member and Administrative Councilman of Southview United Methodist Church.

Lloyd G. Prescott
58 Mahwah Drive
Newark, New Jersey 07430
(201) 555-5297

EDUCATION

Purdue University, 1978
B.S. Industrial Management (minor - Industrial Engineering), GPA: 4.6/6.0.

EMPLOYMENT SUMMARY

Approximately 15 years experience in Industrial Engineering and Manufacturing Process Engineering. Duties have included methods standards, cost reductions, layout, troubleshooting floor production problems, upgrade of equipment, automation, equipment justification, and line balancing. Worked with manufacturing operations involving plastics molding, metal fabrication/assembly, finishing/painting, machining, and casting/rod mill operations.

EMPLOYMENT

8/88 to present:	**Central Engineering**, Newark, NJ Senior Industrial Engineer
1/88 to 8/88:	**Newark Steel and Wire Company**, Newark, NJ Industrial Engineer
7/87 to 12/87:	**Chicago Engineering**, Chicago, IL Contracted Industrial Engineer
4/84 to 5/87:	**Northern Design**, Chicago, IL Industrial Engineer
9/78 to 4/84:	**Industrial Designers**, South Bend, IN Industrial/Process Engineer

ACCOMPLISHMENTS

*   Developed process for assembly and fabrication departments.
*   Conceptualized and drew layouts and tooling for assembly and fabrication.
*   Managed Material Review Board.
*   Established annual budget and monthly manning for line operations.
*   Coordinated cost reduction program.

NOLAN BRIAN KERR
930 North Leland Road
Flint, Michigan 48502
(313) 555-7623

CAREER OBJECTIVE

Position that requires technical knowledge in the areas of design, testing, and reliability of mechanical and electrical systems in order to produce a quality product.

EDUCATION

Purdue University, West Lafayette, Indiana
Attended: August 1982 - June 1985
Bachelor and Associate degrees in Mechanical Engineering Technology.

Indiana State University, Terre Haute, Indiana
Attended: August 1980 - May 1982

Education included 20 hours of electronics and 10 hours of computer programming.

WORK EXPERIENCE

Michigan Lighting, Manufacturing Engineer.
M.L. is a joint American and Japanese automotive lighting company. Experience includes: component designs, thermoset and thermoplastic molding, tooling, material evaluation, assembly line set-ups, adhesive development, robot feasibilities, and customer/supplier contacts. Familiar with foreign and domestic manufacturing concepts. Received Taguchi Design of Experiments Training.

Mercury Lamp Division of Ford Motor Company, Project Engineer.
Five years experience in working with automotive lighting systems. Performed several functions including: developing tests and implementing changes from test car and laboratory data; setting up inventory systems; maintaining budget, timing, and payroll records on computer; designing hardware parts for lamps; coordinating prototype parts; and designing layouts for the Forward Lighting facility. Supervised laboratory technicians, published testing manuals and reports, performed cost savings analysis on computer, and developed systems to monitor product performance in the field.

REFERENCES

Furnished upon request.

DENNIS P. WARDEN
152 Hogarth Avenue
Apt. #7D
Flushing, NY 11367
(718) 555-5401

BUSINESS EXPERIENCE

4/91 to 10/93 -   Industrial Engineer, Needham Cable
Flushing, NY

* Assisted with world class manufacturing and cell technologies implementation for rapid and continual improvement.
* Designed and programmed computerized suggestion system using dBase III reducing clerical duties.
* Coordinated cost reduction program.

10/88 to 9/90 -   Plant Industrial Engineer, Coastal Cable
New Orleans, LA

* Justified and submitted cost reduction projects.
* Served as project engineer for OSHA safety project supervising completion of the project on time and under budget.
* Designed spreadsheet and data base programs to create monthly master production schedules and material requirements for capacity analysis and JIT planning.

6/87 to 8/88 -   Plant Industrial Engineer, Lawrence Metals
Tampa, FL

* Established engineering standards to increase productivity.
* Reduced scrap and rejected shipments by writing detailed process sheets for operator use.

EDUCATION

Columbia University, 1986
School of Engineering and Applied Science
B.S. Mechanical Engineering

Curtis S. Peeler
86 El Camino Real
Austin, Texas 75090

Office: (214) 555-7690   Home: (214) 555-8929

OBJECTIVE: MIS management position with upward potential.

SUMMARY: Outstanding track record:

- o   Management acceptance
- o   Vendor negotiations
- o   Systems/Programming/Operations·
- o   Plan and policy formation

TECHNICAL: DL1/IMS, DOS/VSE, IBM 37U/43xx, CICS, OS/MVS,
Cobol, Fortran, Mark IV, Datamanager.

APPLICATIONS: Distribution, finance, manufacturing, marketing, operations.

EXPERIENCE:

1977-Present   **IBM Corporation**
Austin, Texas

Manager--Customer Administrative Systems (1984-present)

Managing multinational staff on enhancement and implementation of equipment order, control and invoicing COBOL systems developed by IBM in Europe for Latin American operations.

- o   Evaluated and recommended acquisition.
- o   Prepared cost/benefit ROI.
- o   Created project organization requirements.

Manager--Business Systems (1979-1984)

Directed project managers on joint applications development for major subsidiaries, and created plans.   Retained Manager/Systems Applications responsibility.

- o   Programmed, purchased, or transferred applications via formal development and project methodologies.
- o   Conducted overseas management reviews and sold improvement ideas.
- o   Established centralized systems development staff in major local company.

Manager--Systems Application (1977-1979)

Established and managed Systems, Programming, and Operations for Group HQ.

Sher Poona
48 Lawrence Hall
University of California
Berkeley, CA 94720
(510) 555-0568

OBJECTIVE   Development of computer and communication networks.

EDUCATION   University of California at Berkeley
Berkeley, CA
M.S. Electrical Engineering, December 1993
GPA: 3.8/4.0

Chambal Regional College of Engineering
Kanpur, India
B.S. Electrical Engineering, May 1992
Senior Project: Simulated a PC-based protection relay and verified various algorithms for line and phase faults on power transmission lines.

One-month industrial training at Delhi Electronics Limited, Lahore, India, in the areas of data processing, communication, and electronics.

BACKGROUND   Design, modeling, and analysis of centralized and distributed networks, routing and flow algorithms, switching techniques, multiple access for broadcast networks, data communication hardware and software, packet-switched and circuit-switched networks, and satellite and local area networks.

Scientific Programming on VMS, UNIX, and MS-DOS in C, Pascal, Fortran77, Basic, and Assembly Languages.

EXPERIENCE

Adjunct Lecturer, Department of Computer Science, University of California at Berkeley. Instructor for an undergraduate course in FORTRAN programming. (1/93 to 7/93)

ACTIVITIES   **Treasurer**, IEEE Student Chapter, Kanpur, India (1990-1991)
Coordinator, National Symposium on Applications of Telecommunication in the Indian context, Kanpur, India (September 1992)

JAMES B. WEITZMAN
980 CARPENTER ROAD
BUFFALO, NEW YORK 14208
(716) 555-3026

Objective	To obtain employment within your company with the possibility of advancement.

Employment Experience

Aug. 1988 - Present	Baldwin Lumber Company, Buffalo, New York Estimator/Designer - Prepare takeoffs of roof and floor trusses for single and multifamily dwellings as well as commercial and institutional structures. Work requires the ability to read and understand all types of architectural drawings and to develop working roof or floor designs that meet the architect's requirements and the owner's budget.
Jan. 1986 - Feb. 1988	GMA Builders Inc., Rochester, New York Estimator/Draftsman/Computer Operator - Estimated and designed custom homes. Developed an estimating method using the computer to increase efficiency and accuracy of residential estimating.

Education

1978-1980	Rochester Technical Institute, Rochester, New York Graduated from the Associate Degree program in Architectural Engineering Technology with honors. Courses included Technical Math, Physics, Estimating, Basic Engineering, and Architectural Drawing.
1979-1983	Batavia Consolidated High School, Rochester, New York Courses included English, Drafting, History, and Science.
References	Available upon request.
Salary Requirements	Open.

CHARLES W. WHITE
45 Cedar Pines Lane
Logan, Utah 84322
(801) 555-7516

<u>OBJECTIVE</u>	Capitalize on my experience in surveying and develop new skills in related fields.
<u>EDUCATION</u>	UTAH STATE, Logan, Utah Bachelor of Science Degree in Earth Science, May 1987.

<u>AREAS OF</u>
<u>KNOWLEDGE</u>

Physical Geography	Meteorology
Chemistry	Geomorphology
Structural Geology	Glacial Geology
Mineralogy	Oceanography
Calculus	Physics
Wave Optics	Petrology
Paleontology	Astronomy

<u>WORK EXPERIENCE</u>

1/90-1/93	L. HARVEY WILL, Logan, Utah - Party Chief Responsible for three-person crews. Work involved new subdivisions, construction layout, grade work, roads, boundary surveys, stakeouts, and title and deed research.
3/89-1/90	PRICE AND CASPER, Ogden, Utah - Party Chief Performed surveys of residential and commercial property.
9/88-3/89	L. HARVEY WILL, Logan, Utah - Transit Man
1/88-9/88	ROBERT BECK & ASSOCIATES, Provo, Utah - Assistant Surveyor Participated in field work utilizing theodolite and transit, aerial photographs, tax maps, deeds, and sophisticated field instruments.
<u>ACTIVITIES</u>	Back-packed throughout China 6/87-1/88.
<u>INTERESTS</u>	Hiking, tennis, lacrosse, skiing, rock collecting, and traveling.
<u>REFERENCES</u>	Furnished upon request: Office of Career Services, Career Center, Utah State, Logan, UT 84320.

51

RESUME OF PAUL J. RICHARDS
3300 WESTWOOD DRIVE
CUYAHOGA FALLS, OHIO 44221
(216) 555-6929

OBJECTIVE

TO ATTAIN A POSITION AS A DESIGNER DRAFTSMAN WITH A HIGHLY AGGRESSIVE ARCHITECTURAL ENGINEERING FIRM.

SKILLS

DESIGN AND DETAILING OF COMMERCIAL MECHANICAL, ELECTRICAL, AND PLUMBING SYSTEMS. ARCHITECTURAL PLAN AND DETAILS AND SITE LAYOUT.

EXPERIENCE

APRIL 1988 TO PRESENT

THE INDUSTRIAL DESIGN GROUP INC.
DESIGN DEVELOPMENT OF MECHANICAL, ELECTRICAL AND PLUMBING SYSTEMS WITHIN COMMERCIAL PROJECTS. PRODUCE FINAL BID DOCUMENTS ON MULTIPLE MEDIAS AND AUTOCAD SOFTWARE. DEVELOP CONSTRUCTION DETAILS FOR ARCHITECTURAL AND ENGINEERING CONCEPTS. RESPONSIBLE FOR PICTORIAL SECTIONS USED IN SITE DEVELOPMENT AND LAYOUT.

SEPTEMBER 1984 TO MARCH 1988

TACO BELL
SUPERVISED AND EVALUATED THE PERFORMANCE OF 20 EMPLOYEES. SCHEDULED EMPLOYEES TO MAINTAIN A PRODUCTIVE OPERATION. RESPONSIBLE FOR PAYROLL, DAILY AND MONTHLY ACCOUNTING, AND INVENTORY CONTROL

EDUCATION

CLEVELAND INSTITUTE OF APPLIED SCIENCES
MECHANICAL DESIGN AND DRAFTING TECHNOLOGY 12/88
PURSUING B.S. IN MECHANICAL ENGINEERING TECHNOLOGY

INTERESTS

HOME IMPROVEMENT, SKIING, AND BASEBALL.

REFERENCES

AVAILABLE UPON REQUEST.

Scott Monroe
64 Fountain Lake Road
Gary, IN 46408
(219) 555-6823

Title:	**ELECTRICAL ENGINEER/POWER DEMAND/MAINTENANCE**

Education: BSEE, 1986, Purdue University, GPA 3.5/4.0.
MS Electrical Engineering, 1990, Northwestern University,
GPA 3.6/4.0.

Experience:

BETHLEHEM STEEL, Gary, IN

1989-present AREA MANAGER-STEELMAKING RELIABILITY
Supervise salary and nonsalary positions. Implemented and developed a
new power demand system and new vacuum system.

1988-1989 STEEL OPERATIONS MAINTENANCE ENGINEER
Supervised combustion, electrical, and electronics engineering.
Investigated and solved electrical and mechanical problems.

1987-1988 SUPERVISOR-STEELMAKING RELIABILITY
Responsible for regular and preventative maintenance of steelmaking
equipment. Interfaced with support group and contractors.

1986-1987 ASSOCIATE MANUFACTURING ENGINEER
Investigated furnace transformer failures. Incorporated new technology.

1985 **ALLENTOWN STEEL**, Pittsburgh, PA
ELECTRICAL ENGINEER
Installed quality control x-ray system. Designed and installed an
automatic conveyor system.

1983-1984 **GOODYEAR TIRE & RUBBER CO.**, Akron, OH
ELECTRICAL ENGINEER
Assisted in installation of new test wheel. Installed twelve new tire
presses.

References: Available upon request.

EDGAR PETERS
9 DeSoto Drive
Baton Rouge, LA 70805
(504) 555-1388

OBJECTIVE: Industrial Engineering position with
                    involvement in a manufacturing
                    environment and opportunities to advance
                    into production management.

EDUCATION: Master of Engineering
                    Tulane University, 1986
                    Major: Industrial Engineering

                    Bachelor of Science
                    Tulane University, 1985

EXPERIENCE:
1986 to present   Alexander Steel Company, Baton Rouge, LA

                    Associate Industrial Engineer
                    Provide identification and
                    implementation of computer applications
                    for analysis and control. Activities
                    include computer modeling and economic
                    and statistical analysis. Originated an
                    operating change to increase furnace hot
                    blast temperature. Developed
                    diagnostic, routing, quality control and
                    unit scheduling expert systems.

1985 to 1986   Packaging Systems Inc., New Orleans, LA

                    Part-time Supervisor
                    Responsible for 10 people in package
                    sort activities. Supervised, evaluated,
                    and trained sort and audit personnel.

1983 to 1985   Production Facilities, New Orleans, LA

                    Student Assistant
                    Assisted project managers in development
                    of new production and test facilities.
                    Developed and documented procedures for
                    initiating component repairs.

REFERENCES: Available upon request.

BRYAN PULLMAN
43 BUFFALO BILL ROAD
OMAHA, NE 68129
(402) 555-5837

EDUCATION

- University of Nebraska at Lincoln, 1988
  B.S. Geology
- University of Nebraska at Lincoln
  Graduate studies in Geology, Forestry, and Natural Resources

PROFESSIONAL EXPERIENCE

<u>Project Geologist</u>
Buckman & Klein Engineering Inc., 4/89 - present
- Manage environmental assessments for properties undergoing acquisition, divesture, or refinancing.
- Supervise and document underground storage tank removal and subsequent contaminated soil remediation.
- Designed soil venting systems, groundwater recovery/treatment systems, and bioremediation programs.
- Responsible for proposals, drill scheduling, material purchasing, invoicing, and client development on projects.

RELEVANT EXPERIENCE

<u>Materials Engineering Technician</u>
Maxwell Associates, 5/88 - 4/89

<u>Engineering Assistant</u>
Nebraska Department of Natural Resources Division of Water, 2/88 - 4/88

ACHIEVEMENTS

- Nebraska Academy of Science - Presented and published "The Formation of the Platte Sinkhole and the Drainage Effects on Platte and Stapleton Hollows."
- Geological Society of America - Presented research project on soil development at 1988 convention.

Lionel Dean
46 Bay Drive
Chicago, IL 60641
(312) 555-7862

**CAREER
OBJECTIVE**

A mechanical engineering position in a manufacturing/design environment.

EDUCATION

B.S., Mechanical Engineering Technology
University of Illinois at Urbana/Champaign
Major G.P.A. - 4.8/5.0, December 1987

EXPERIENCE

1988 to Present

UNITED STATES STEEL, East Chicago, IN

HYDRAULIC/MAINTENANCE ENGINEER

Hydraulic Engineer assigned as mechanical coordinator for modernization project.

Responsibilities include hydraulic system design, purchasing of equipment, drawing approval, updating hydraulic schematics for revamp projects, and development of a hydraulic training program for mechanical maintenance personnel.

Maintenance Engineer responsible for the design, procurement, and construction of various mechanical/structural projects.

Duties include development and estimate of work, selection of an engineering contractor, scheduling and cost control, development of contractor bid packages, selection of a field contractor, and overall approval and supervision of field work.

MAINTENANCE TURN FOREMAN

Responsibilities included supervision of bargaining unit employees who maintained a flat roll steel finishing facility.

1983 to 1987

UNIVERSITY GROUP, Urbana, IL

MAINTENANCE SUPERVISOR

Responsibilities included repair and operation of HVAC, building utilities, grounds, and their respective equipment.

PERSONAL RESUME

NAME: Leslie J. Mitchell

ADDRESS: 7985 Scott Road, Indianapolis, IN 46240

TELEPHONE: 317-555-4641

OBJECTIVE: To obtain a position in the field of interior architecture.

DESIGN EXPERIENCE:

1989-Present	Facility Planner/Interior Designer, Designtree Business Interiors, Inc. Indianapolis, IN. Responsible for space planning facilities and offices. Steelcase trained with CAP, AutoCad, and Intergraph.
1988-1989	Interior Designer, The Smythe Group, Indianapolis, IN. Responsible for construction documentation, space planning, and presentation boards.
1987-1988	Design Consultant, Nile Engineering Corporation, Fort Wayne, IN. Responsible for space planning construction documentation, project management, and material selection.
1987	Design Consultant, Indiana Architects, Inc., Fort Wayne, IN. Responsible for space planning and designing and creating renderings for presentation boards.
1985-1986	Interior Designer, Design Services, Anderson, IN. Designed residential homes with architect-partner. Responsible for interior design and material selection.
1984-1985	Designed and remodeled private residences and offices, Singapore.

EDUCATION: Ball State University
B.S. Environmental Design Studies - 1984

REFERENCES: Furnished on request.

Mark Chang
587 Flint Drive
Detroit, MI 48202
(313) 555-3578

Objective   To obtain a position as an engineer where I can apply my knowledge of digital circuit design, programmable controllers,and microprocessors.

Employment   Chrysler Data Systems
Detroit, MI
Systems Engineer - Initially worked at Chrysler's LeBaron Division with the Electrical/HVAC Group resolving computer problems, keeping inventory, and establishing the goals of the group. Then worked at Chrysler's Powertrain plant as part of the Plant Floor Systems Group resolving problems, analyzing change requests, and writing troubleshooting documentation for an automated storage and retrieval system. July 1992 to November 1993.

Perkins Engineering
Flint, MI
Die Detailer - Responsibilities included drawing and dimensioning die details, making engineering changes to die drawings and details, and running blueprints. May 1990 to November 1991.

Education   Michigan State University, East Lansing, MI Bachelor of Science degree in Electrical Engineering, May 1992. GPA: 3.2/4.0. Computer Languages: Assembly, Fortran, Basic. Relevant Courses: Programmable Controllers, Digital Circuit Design, Microprocessors, Automotive Electronics.

Passed the Professional Engineering Exam, April 1992.

Affiliations   Institute of Electrical and Electronic Engineers

References   Available upon request.

WILLIAM J. SHAW

1810 Cedar Crest Boulevard
Evansville, IN 47722
(812) 555-1379

CAREER SUMMARY

Over 20 years experience in manufacturing, production, and assembly of medium- and high-volume stamping and fabrication operations. Supervised activities in fabrication, stamping, welding, and finishing of automotive and agricultural equipment as well as appliances. Responsible for training, scheduling, safety, work quality, material movement, and discipline.

TECHNICAL QUALIFICATIONS

Experienced with JIT, MRP, Statistical Process control, and automated visual inventory/scheduling concepts. Proficient in high speed light stampings, transfer press operations, heavy stamped assemblies, welding, and testing instrumentation/procedures.

EMPLOYMENT HISTORY

Whirlpool Corporation, Evansville, IN   8/86 to present
Operations/Finishing Manager

Ford Motor Company, San Leandro, CA   6/74 to 8/86
Positions held: Supervisor of Cab Fabrication/Finishing, Maintenance Supervisor, and Finished Vehicle Assembly Supervisor.

Blue Mountain Appliances, Pittsburgh, PA   1967 to 1974
Positions held: Shipping Supervisor, Senior Quality Technician, and Rotating Shift Supervisor.

EDUCATION

B.S. Business Administration, Carnegie Mellon University, 1984

Available upon request.

Rachel Schwartzman
125 College Way
Princeton, NJ 08545
(609) 555-2956

Objective: Mechanical engineering and/or programming position involving robotics or other electromechanical systems.

Education: **Princeton University**, Princeton, NJ
Major: Mechanical Engineering (GPA: 3.8/4.0)
1990 - present
Won undergraduate research fellowship to perform independent robotics research.

Experience:

Summer 1993 *Programmer.* **General Electric (Robotics Lab)**
Developed a robotic work cell using Linear-Motor-Robots to assemble washer-pumps at high production rates. Designed the gripper hardware for each task in the production cycle as well as designing all the fixturing for the parts being assembled.

Summer 1992 *Mechanical Engineer.* **Ford Motor Company**
Designed an integrated car seat frame which used hydraulics to absorb much of the impact energy in an accident. Also, designed a power window motor casing to facilitate robotic assembly of window systems on assembly line.

Summer 1991 *Computer Programmer.* **World Airways, Inc.**
Set up monthly customer mailing system/inventory data base in D-Base and Pascal.

Summer 1990 *Robotics/Computer Programmer.* **Rutgers University**
Programmed Robotic Lab equipment and vision system for horticulture research.

Awards and Honors:

General Electric Scholarship: full-tuition
Member, Tau Beta Pi
Member, Phi Beta Kappa

MARGARET H. MINGER
P.O. Box 714
St. Joseph, MO 64507
(816) 555-4268

PROFESSIONAL OBJECTIVE:

To work in a position that will enable me to gain additional experience in construction and construction management.

EXPERIENCE:

May 1991 to
  Present

Project Administrator
Eagle Constructors - St. Joseph, Missouri
Reconstruction of a cold storage and controlled atmosphere facility. As-built drawing updates, change order processing, overall document control and tracking to establish owner-caused delays, processing and tracking of submittals, and schedule generation and updating.

May 1989 to
May 1991

Assistant Field Engineer
MRSS Constructors - Carbondale, Missouri
Missouri State Prison. Mobilization of project site office, assisted in design review efforts of bid packages, personnel training in construction document processing procedures, as-built drawing updates, change order estimating, punchlist tracking, and project closeout.

April 1986 to
January 1991

Assistant Field Engineer
MRSS Constructors - Fulton, Missouri
Missouri State Prison. Processing, maintaining, and tracking of PCO's and change orders for each contractor on site; authored and assembled a closeout procedures manual; processing and tracking of submittals; and ultimately sole responsibility for closeout.

EDUCATION:

Washington University - St. Louis, Missouri
B.S. in December 1991, GPA: 3.9
Major: Construction Management

MEMBERSHIPS:

National Association of Women in Construction
Students in Construction
Sigma Lambda Chi, National Honor society for construction students

AWARDS AND HONORS:

Nominated Dean's Medalist, 1990-1991
Outstanding Student in the Department of Industrial Technology, 1990-1991
Outstanding Student in Industrial Technology/Construction, 1990-1991

REFERENCES:

Available upon request.

VERNON GILLESPIE
461 Pike Drive
Denver, Colorado 80236
(303) 555-8446

EDUCATION

B.S. - Construction Management, May 1984, GPA 3.5
Colorado School of Mines

Journeyman Carpenter Certification, August, 1993

PROFESSIONAL EXPERIENCE

1991-1993   Carpenter-Union Local No. 5555 Denver, Apprenticeship Program
Employers:
      Louis G. Perez, Inc. - Denver, CO
      Collins Construction Company - Denver, CO
      Construction Specialties, Inc. - Fort Collins, CO
      The Davies Company - Boulder, CO

1988-1991   Construction Administrator
G.T. Salt, Inc. - Greeley, CO
      Responsible for estimating and material procurement on various industrial and commercial projects in Sterling and Platte Counties.

1984-1987   Project Engineer
Golden Construction Company, Inc. - Golden, CO
      Responsible for estimating, bidding, and managing general engineering and utility type projects including: fiber optic cable installation for AT&T and refinery work at Chevron U.S.A. and Shell Oil.

RELATED SKILLS

Subcontractor Coordination   Bidding
Budgeting and Cost Control   CPM Scheduling
Journeyman Level Carpenter   Estimating

Morris G. Hampden
8 Sydney Road
Fairfax, Virginia 22030
Home: (703) 555-2109
Work: (703) 555-9067

PROFESSIONAL OBJECTIVE:
To excel in a construction management position by drawing knowledge from field experience and utilizing modern management techniques.

PROFESSIONAL EXPERIENCE:

July 1990 to Present

Granite Construction Co.
Washington, DC
TUNNEL CONCRETE ENGINEER
Participated in planning of concrete activity considering concurrent design/review/approval process requiring frequent course changes. Conceived and managed redesign of unworkable tunnel form system, material delivery scheduling, production of lift drawings, and draft material submittals.

June 1989 to July 1990

Granite Construction Co.
Fresno, CA
CIVIL ENGINEER
Handled quantity take-off and estimated and planned tunnel construction.

Summers 1986, 87, 88
1984 to 1985

Sierra Consultants
San Francisco, CA
SURVEY PARTY CHIEF
Roads, sewer and water lines, small structures; quantity calculations; and drafting.

PROFESSIONAL:

Licenses:

Engineer-in-Training, California
Surveyor-in-Training, California
Certified Concrete Testing Tech., ACI

Organizations:

American Society of Civil Engineers

ANA FONG
1260 PALMETTO DRIVE
ORLANDO, FL 32816
(305) 555-1318

OBJECTIVE

To utilize my management, marketing, and computer service experiences to make an immediate contribution as a member of a professional management team.

TECHNICAL EXPERTISE

SYSTEMS: CA/1, CA/7, CICS, MVS/XA, Vtam, SUPRA

HARDWARE: IBM 309X - 308X, IBM 4331, StorageTek 4400 ACS

EMPLOYMENT SUMMARY

CORPORATE OPERATIONS MANAGER   1984-1993
REYNOLDS CORPORATION   Orlando, FL

- **Directed** implementation of new data center and hired and trained operations and network personnel.

- **Installed** corporate telecommunications systems including PBX's and key systems.

- **Coordinated** hardware acquisitions and lease negotiations for all nationwide corporate facilities.

- **Reduced** printing costs by managing a project team through the analysis, design, development, and implementation of new printing systems and procedures.

OPERATIONS MANAGER   1981-1984
DADE COUNTY INFORMATION SERVICES AGENCY   Miami, FL

- **Initiated** automated problem resolution system resulting in reduction of problems and elimination of manual system.

- **Developed** position titles and pay scales which resulted in identifiable career paths for operations personnel.

ANA FONG **page 2**

EDUCATION

University of California at Los Angeles
B.S. Computer Science, 1981

AFFILIATIONS

- Florida Telecommunications User Association
- Association for Computer Operations Managers
- Reynolds Corporate Mentor for Partners in Education Program

REFERENCES

Available upon request.

PETER DAWSON

420 Calumet Avenue, Gary, IN 46408 219/555/6457

OBJECTIVE

Position in process metallurgy/quality control.

CAREER SUMMARY

Fifteen years service with a major manufacturer of flat-rolled and tubular products in various functional areas. Highly developed skills in work organization, metallurgical process control and applications, and expertise in finishing and management of basic manufacturing.

WORK EXPERIENCE

United States Steel Corporation, Gary, IN   **1986 - Present**

Hot Mill Metallurgist (1988 - present)
Responsible for all aspects of hot strip mill quality including mill thermal practice, customer product and processing requirements, testing, and claims.

- Established new product/grade hot-rolling standards.
- Supervised hot strip mill quality control work force, including metallurgical turn foreman, observers, and testing personnel.

High Carbon/Alloy Metallurgist (1986 - 1988)
Responsible for quality and thermal process control for all high carbon and alloy grades/products.

- Directed and coordinated slabbing and hot-rolling of customer conversion material.
- Established and developed standard operating and testing procedures for high-tech alloy application.

United States Steel Corporation, Cleveland, OH   **1978-1986**

Shipping Supervisor (1984 - 1986)
Responsible for coordinating and scheduling all finishing operations.

Finishing Supervisor (1978 -1983)
Responsible for processing of various sizes, lengths, and grades of tubular products.

EDUCATION

B.S. Metallurgical Engineering, Purdue University, West Lafayette, IN, 1978

DAVID FORTSON

1038 Independence Drive • Dayton, OH 45469 • (513) 555-4429

PROFESSIONAL OBJECTIVE

Senior Software Engineer with responsibility for both small and large software projects from conceptual phase to finished product.

TECHNICAL EXPERTISE

HARDWARE: FORCE 68030, SUN Workstation, DEC VAX, HP 9000, IBM AT 386, DEC LS1 1140/44

OPERATING SYSTEMS: UNIX, VMS, VXWORKS, MS-DOS, VERSADOS

LANGUAGES: C, MACRO Assembler, FORTRAN, BASIC, ASYST

EXPERIENCE

Automatic Optical Systems   1989 – Present
Columbus, OH

<u>Senior Software Engineer</u> – Responsible for detailed specifications, detailed designs, implementation, and maintenance of the software that controls and acquires data from a real time experimental laser system. Key duties include providing software specification reviews for internal and external audiences.

o   Integrated and implemented hardware/software system to acquire low and high speed data from different sensor channels.

o   Implemented complex mathematical algorithms used to control the laser system and to provide diagnostic information. Working under the direction of the chief research physicist.

Software, Inc.   1988
Dayton, OH

<u>Senior Software Engineer</u> – Performed software engineering services as a consultant for employers. Designed, developed, and debugged assembly language code for DEC VAX system performing on-line cellular telephone caller validation.

o   Developed new code and modified existing code to decrease the time required to verify cellular telephone caller's identity.

DAVID FORTSON

OTX Y Systems   1985 - 1988
Dayton, OH

<u>Senior Engineer</u> - Responsible for design and implementation of software high visibility national defense software projects.

o   Worked as team leader and senior contributing member of several hardware/software design teams. Wrote software requirement specifications based upon DOD 2167A protocol. Comprehensive customer interface and design reviews were required.

o   Designed, developed, and implemented software that was part of an HP9000 based Automatic Test System in conjunction with hardware designers and manufacturing engineering.

Cardinal Distribution   1978 - 1985
Cincinnati, OH

<u>Senior Engineer</u> - Responsible for the design and development of software units that were used in many different parts of the Digital Central Office Telephone system.

o   Wrote software that implemented extensive fault detection and isolation techniques in order to guarantee the integrity of the on-line call processing system.

o   Produced the software that allowed the direct interface of the company's central office equipment to the AT&T network.

o   Provided round the clock customer software support.

EDUCATION

B.S., Miami University, Oxford, OH

Currently enrolled in the MS Computer Science Software Engineering program, Ohio State University, Columbus, OH

RESUME

OF

STEPHANIE MORRIS

ADDRESS/PHONE:

11917 North Meridian
Carmel, IN 46032
(317) 555-6463

OBJECTIVE:

Seeking a challenging position in the areas of systems
analysis, data base management, and programming that
will utilize my technical and interpersonal skills.

EDUCATION:

University of Texas
Austin, Texas
B.S. Computer Technology, Computer Information Systems
Minors - Business, Industrial Operations
Fall, 1980 - Fall, 1985

WORK EXPERIENCE:

Carl James Associates, Indianapolis, Indiana
Associate (February 1987 to Present)
Converted all operations for an Indiana municipality
from Burroughs ISAM/COBOL/RPG to HP3000 IMAGE/COOL.
Redesigned, rewrote, developed, and implemented all
applications and new development.

Mayflower Van Lines, Indianapolis, Indiana
Programmer/Analyst (February 1986 - February 1987)
Designed, developed and implemented reporting
applications for operations including financial and
operational reporting. Responsible for PC hardware and
software set up and support for 25 PCs. Provided user
support for applications written in FOCUS on an Amdahl
mainframe.

Hardware Wholesalers, South Bend, Indiana
Programmer/Analyst Trainee (Summer 1985)
Programmed COBOL with IDMS, created an on-line
application using CICS and COBOL, and wrote
documentation and created new applications using
Easytrieve Plus and Keymaster.

STEPHANIE MORRIS

TECHNICAL SKILLS:

Languages
- COBOL
- BASIC
- RPG II
- Assembly

Fourth Generation Languages
- PROTOS
- Cognos Powerhouse
- FOCUS

Environments
- DOS/VSE
- MPE
- VM/CMS

Data Base Management Systems
- IMAGE
- ADABAS
- IDMS

Hardware
- HP3000
- IBM 30XX, 43XX
- DC PDP 11/70
- IBM PC/AT

Application Areas
- Order Processing
- Payroll Processing
- Records Management

- Work Order Processing
- Financials Processing

NONTECHNICAL SKILLS:

Verbal Communications
- Interpersonal
- Presentations
- Speeches

Written Communications
- Feasibility Studies
- Technical Reports
- Project Documentation
- Design Specifications

REFERENCES AVAILABLE UPON REQUEST

JED ORR, JR.

68 Desert Palm Lane
Tulsa, Oklahoma 74175
(918) 555-4623

EDUCATION

The University of Oklahoma, Norman, Oklahoma
B.S. Computer Science (April 1985)
Minor: Mathematics

EMPLOYMENT HISTORY

The Ryland Organization, Aviation Training Services
5450 West 5th Street
Tulsa, Oklahoma 74171

Position:	Contractor
Software:	CLIPPER vSummer '87, DBASE III+, Turbo C v2.1, Novell Netware, BRIEF, UNIX
Hardware:	Gateway 2000 386SX, Zenith Z-248, AST 386/25, IBM PC-XT, Leading Edge PC-XT
Employment Dates:	June 1988 to December 1993

Ogden Investment Incorporated
1265 Lincoln Boulevard, Suite 901
Potomac, Maryland 20854

Position:	Programmer/Analyst
Software:	CLIPPER vSummer '87, DBASE III+, Novell Netware, Norton Utilities
Hardware:	Standard 286
Employment Dates:	April 1988 to June 1988

Northwest Airlines Flight Center
Minneapolis International Airport
Edina, Minnesota 55435

Position:	Programmer/Analyst
Software:	CLIPPER vSummer '87, DBASE II and III, POWER C, BRIEF, MPAS, CP/M, PC-DOS
Hardware:	Zenith Z-241 and Z-248, IBM PC-XT
Employment Dates:	December 1985 to April 1988

Jed Orr, Jr.

Center for Technology
University of Tulsa
Tulsa, Oklahoma, 74104
Position: Programming Team Manager
Software: TUTOR, NOS
Hardware: CDC Cyber 730, IST-III, Viking 720
Employment Dates: January 1985 to December 1985

Michael G. Block   Home: (617) 555-4813
75 Eldridge Court   Work: (617) 555-6741
Cambridge, MA 02138

OBJECTIVE: To utilize my communication, problem-solving, and decision-
                  making skills in a professional position which offers development
                  and increasing levels of responsibility.

EDUCATION: Ivy Technical Institute - Associate Degree
                  Material Requirements Planning Seminars - Certificate
                  ITT Technical Institute - Certificate

EXPERIENCE:

10/89 - Present   Lincoln Engineering - Cambridge, MA
                  Service Technician Assistant - Assist service technicians in
                  installing heating and air conditioning units in various city-wide
                  industrial and residential applications. Provide pick-up and
                  delivery service. Operate hydraulic forklift. Use acetylene/oxygen
                  cutting torch and other related trade tools.

4/84 - 9/89   Taylor Components Group - Concord, NH
                  Programmer Technician - Developed and maintained applications
                  for various departments. Created screen formats for program
                  access using FOCUS Report Writer language.

                  Trainer - Provided end users with working understanding of
                  computer. Taught in-house seminar on creating Bills-of-Material
                  using Cullinet on-line software package.

                  Help Service - Allocated, created, and deleted data sets for end
                  users. Provided troubleshooting assistance. Served as liaison
                  between Management Information Service and various departments.

                  Documentation - Prepared and provided end users with step-by-step
                  procedures for using computer. Prepared user manual for Bills-of-
                  Materials seminar.

4/79 - 3/84   Taylor Components Group - Concord, NH
                  Draftsman - Prepared detailed drawings of parts from layouts and
                  sketches using standard drawings and drafting and measuring tools
                  and instruments.

<u>RESUME</u>

Robert L. Montgomery
46 Washington Boulevard
Albuquerque, New Mexico 87131
(505) 555-3315

<u>EDUCATION</u>:   BS Civil Engineering 1967
                University of California, Berkeley

<u>EXPERIENCE</u>:   KAISER HEAVY CONSTRUCTION
                4200 Santa Fe Drive
                Albuquerque, New Mexico 87134

6/84 to 5/93   Senior Estimator in home office. Handled all
                underground bids.

9/83 to 6/84   Special Projects Engineer on King Dam
                Project. Supervised excavation of
                underground powerhouse.

                MONTGOMERY, INC.
                46 Washington Boulevard
                Albuquerque, New Mexico 87131

1/81 to 9/83   Consultant to heavy construction contractors
                on estimating, claim preparation,
                construction management, and design of ground
                support systems.

                Consultant to law firms on preparation of
                legal proceedings involving construction
                claims.

4/78 to 1/81   Subcontractor doing pipe jacking, small
                tunnels, bulkhead and stone revetments,
                structure grouting, grading, and sitework.

                R & G CONSTRUCTORS, INC
                8715 Highway 395
                Reno, Nevada 89557

10/73 to 10/75 Project Engineer on Emigrant Gap Tunnel,
                South Lake Tahoe, California.

EXPERIENCE: R & G CONSTRUCTORS, INC.

2/75 to 4/78   Project Engineer on relief sewer in Reno.

DILINGNHAM-GRAVES-GRANITE
General Engineering consultants to
Washington, DC Rapid Transit.
Washington, DC

7/67 to 10/73   Started as Field Engineer and worked up to
Resident Engineer. Involved in the following
work:

2,400 feet of exploratory tunnels.

33,000 feet of tunnel driven by conventional
methods in rock.

7,000 feet of tunnel driven using a boring
machine.

Spent 1-1/2 years as designer on underground
structures.

REGISTRATION: Professional Engineer in the following
states:

New Mexico
District of Columbia
Nevada

KEVIN G. ACKROYD
438 Beaver Drive, Apt. 67
University Park, PA 16802
(814) 555-9478

EMPLOYMENT GOAL

Full-time employment in a medium-sized company that does earthwork and/or heavy construction.

EDUCATION

Penn State University - Senior 1992-93, Graduate June 1993
Degree - Bachelor of Science in Construction Engineering Management

RELATED EXPERIENCE

ENGINEER INTERN - Williamsport Paving Co., Williamsport, PA, June to September 1992. Responsible for upkeep of the job costing system on all projects and time and material billings. Some estimating, job supervision, signing, and laboring.

PROJECT OFFICER - 125th Engineer Battalion, PAANG, 1990 to present. The Officer-In-Charge of a road construction project and a haul-in project. Duties include coordination of materials, equipment, and personnel and direct supervision of project.

GRADE CHECKER/LABOR - White Construction Co., Wilkes-Barre, PA, July to September 1991. Gained experience in grade checking, pipe-laying, chip-seal, and flagging.

EQUIPMENT OPERATOR - Barron's Trenching, Altoona, PA, July to September 1990. Operated a CASE 580 Backhoe and 450 dozer in excavation for farm drainage systems and private contract work.

LEADERSHIP, ACTIVITIES, HONORS & AWARDS

MEMBER - AGC Student Chapter, Penn State
COMMANDER - ROTC Drill Team
PLATOON LEADER - Heavy Equipment Platoon, National Guard
SCHOLARSHIP - AGC, 3-year, undergraduate

KARL DOTY · 35 YORK AVENUE, EDINA, MN 55460 · (612) 555-4161

EXPERIENCE:
Aug. 1986-Present

TUBULAR PRODUCTS   Bloomington, MN
Central Maintenance Supervisor

Responsible for the hydraulic and lubrication
systems of new continuous caster.

March 1986-Aug. 1986

ANOKA, INC.   Minneapolis, MN
Manager Maintenance Services

Responsible for scheduling and direction of
maintenance staff, parts ordering, and inventory
control. Supervised design, fabrication, and
start-up of new equipment.

Oct. 1984-Nov. 1985

TUBULAR PRODUCTS GROUP   Bloomington, MN
Mechanical Department Foreman

Responsible for supervision of hydraulic,
lubrication, and machine mechanics in
troubleshooting and correction of malfunctions.
Completed set-up of machine operations according
to schematics.

Jan. 1981-Oct. 1984

Hydraulic Foreman

Responsible for supervision of 8-man crew who
performed maintenance functions.

Sept. 1976-Jan. 1981

Hydraulic Repairman

Responsible for locating and repairing problems
in various hydraulic equipment. Received
certificates for job-related training in a
complete hydraulic apprentice program.

EDUCATION:
1986-Present

COMMUNITY COLLEGE   Minneapolis, MN
AA in Business Management in December, 1993

Oct. 1987

LUBRICAT CORPORATION   Minneapolis, MN
Certificate in Automated Lubrication Systems

Jan. 1987

LYMAN HYDRAULICS   Bloomington, MN
Certificate in Maintaining Hydraulic Components
& Systems

Oct.-Nov. 1986

"TRAINING IN EUROPE"   Germany and Switzerland
Studied state-of-the-art technology for the
application of hydraulic control and power units

Feb. 1985

UNIVERSITY OF MINNESOTA   Minneapolis, MN
Certificate in Planned Lubrication

May 1985

COMMUNITY COLLEGE   Minneapolis, MN
Certificate in Advanced Industrial Supervision

KARL DOTY   Page 2

ACTIVITIES: Active member of the Hydraulic and Lubrication
                         Committee of the American Iron & Steel Engineers

ACCOMPLISHMENTS: Elected and served as borough councilman for
                         local municipality (1981-1983)

REFERENCES: Available upon request.

RESUME
Leo Cervetto
18 Cliff Road
Portland, Oregon 97205
(503) 555-3546

PROFESSIONAL EXPERIENCE

COORDINATOR OF TECHNICAL SERVICES, ALLIANCE OREGON, INC., DECEMBER 1989 TO PRESENT.

In charge of asbestos programs for over 100 school buildings, involving review of existing asbestos management programs and extensive contact with school administrators in planning and implementation of timely and budget-sensitive management programs for environmental issues.

Regularly conducted field surveillance and inspection activities at all sites. Trained school personnel on various environmental issues including asbestos, lead, and radon.

Wrote company hazard communication, respiratory protection, and medical surveillance programs as well as standard operating procedures manuals for functions within the asbestos management program.

INDUSTRIAL HYGIENIST, ENVIRONMENTAL CONSULTANTS, MARCH 1988 TO OCTOBER 1989.

Project manager position involving coordination of industrial hygiene and asbestos-related projects: Bulk sampling, technical report writing, abatement project specification development, environmental compliance monitoring, and project design. Supervised technician pool and client services.

Carried out wet chemistry procedures applicable to analysis of priority pollutants-organic and inorganic for solid and liquid matrices.

LABORATORY TECHNICIAN, BEAVER ANALYTICAL SERVICES, JUNE 1987 TO FEBRUARY 1988.

Responsible for preparation of solid and liquid samples for the analysis of tetrachlorodibenzodioxin. Duties included sample check-in, solid/liquid extraction, various clean-up procedures, and standards preparation.

EDUCATION

PORTLAND STATE UNIVERSITY, MAY 1987
Bachelor of Science, Biology
Chemistry minor

TRAINING/ACCREDITATION

OSHA compliance training

EPA-accredited building inspector, asbestos

EPA-accredited asbestos management planner, asbestos

Sampling and Evaluating Airborne Asbestos Dust certification

SPECIALTIES

All aspects of asbestos management in residential and commercial buildings

Air sample analysis by Polarized Light Microscopy

Indoor air quality evaluation

Industrial Hygiene sampling

Richard L. Stein
1837 Forest Place
St. Louis, MO 63130
(314) 555-6411

WORK EXPERIENCE

Jefferson Foundry and Machine Company
St. Louis, MO
1988 to Present

Industrial Engineer Manager
Supervised and trained junior industrial engineers.
Performed cost justification and preliminary
engineering of new high technology core and mold
machines. Instituted a comprehensive database
containing procedures, rates, tooling modifications,
dimensional layouts, and quality problems which
ultimately reduced scrap in half. Created tooling
design manuals to assist vendors in constructing new
tooling for foundry equipment. Formed job review teams
to improve the quality and lower the cost of individual
jobs. Improved the cost overhead system, and wrote
software to rapidly update job costs and provide fast
estimated costs. Worked with customer's engineers and
pattern vendors to bring innovative castings of high
quality and lower cost to the market.

Charter Corporation
St. Louis, MO
1985 to 1988

Sales Proposal Engineer
Prepared detailed written quotations and drawings
describing automatic gauging, assembly machines,
complete cells, or systems. Worked in cooperation with
the engineering and manufacturing departments to
establish new machine designs to meet customer
requirements. Estimated pricing based on engineering,
manufacturing, and purchase content.

Jefferson Foundry and Machine Company
St. Louis, MO
1979 to 1985

Industrial Engineer
Methodized production jobs and constructed standard
data with time studies. Prepared job cost estimates
and tooling quotes. Designed and supervised the
construction of an isocure sand heater.

Junior Industrial Engineer
Implemented piecework incentive system in the millroom covering annealing, blast clean, snag, and inspect operations. Set work standard throughout the foundry.

General Tire Company
St. Louis, MO
1978

Production Machinist
Machined, drilled, bored, and inspected castings.

Shasta Motor Homes
St. Louis, MO
1977

Inspector-Finisher
Inspected and repaired defective motor homes.

EDUCATION

Clark Vocational Technical College
Fundamental and Advanced Computer Aided Design, 1985-1986

University of Missouri/Columbia
Advanced Statistical Process Control, 1984
B.S. Degree in Mechanical Engineering Technology, with Distinction, 1983
A.A.S. Degree in Industrial Engineering Technology, with Distinction, 1979
A.A.S. Degree in Mechanical Engineering Technology, with Distinction, 1978

References available upon request.

RESUME
of
MANUEL RUIZ

46 Via Esperanza
La Jolla, CA 92093
Phone: 619-555-7122

EDUCATION

B.S. Safety Management, University of California/San Diego
Minor: Business Administration and Life Science

EMPLOYMENT SUMMARY

Over 14 years experience in safety administration with manufacturing operations. Developed and implemented the following:
- safety rules, procedures, and regulations applicable for manufacturing operations
- new fire alarm and sprinkler system
- safety activities and promotional programs to maintain safety awareness
- contractors' training programs to maintain contractors' safety within the facility

Responsible for security, shift supervision, and lab functions. Successfully managed personnel and department budgets.

ACCOMPLISHMENTS

- Maintained high level of safety for a La Jolla Chemical Corporation plant for 7 years without a lost time injury.
- Assisted and coordinated contractors in cleaning and removing of almost 200 tanks and several miles of piping.
- Assisted in the rebuilding of a dragline with no lost time accidents/injuries.
- Exceeded corporate goals while maintaining plant needs.

EMPLOYMENT

1979 to present   La Jolla Chemical Corporation, San Diego, CA
                   Positions: Safety Manager, Safety Coordinator, and
                   Safety Inspector

WILBUR KENNEDY
619 Alameda Street
Santa Barbara, CA 93107
(805) 555-3428

SUMMARY

Eight years of nuclear operations experience in the U.S. Navy followed by four years of management experience and two years of design experience in electronics industry.

EXPERIENCE

1988 -1993

ACE ELECTRONICS GROUP, Santa Barbara, CA

Engineer   1991-1993

- Designed over 10 optical sensors and industrial controls.
- Designed circuit board layouts.
- Supervised the production and testing of prototypes.
- Supervised the maintenance of engineering department records and drawings.
- Worked with customers to design solutions to their applications.

Production Manager   1989-1991

- Made planning, controlling, and staffing decisions.
- Supervised production of sensors and oscillators.
- Selected and implemented software and hardware for computer accounting of inventory.

Technician   1988-1989

- Tested, adjusted, and repaired optical sensors and crystal oscillators.

1980-1988

U.S. NAVY

Nuclear-powered Research Submarine   1984-1988

- Assigned as Interior Communications Officer and Computer Officer.
- Supervised and maintained underwater closed-circuit television equipment, digital computer equipment, and electronic navigation equipment.

WILBUR KENNEDY - PAGE 2

EXPERIENCE CONT.

Nuclear-powered Submarine   1983-1984

- Operated and maintained electrical generating and distribution equipment.
- Performed vibration analysis of rotating equipment.

EDUCATION/
TRAINING

B.S., Electronic Engineering Technology
University of California, Santa Barbara

USN Nuclear Power School
USN Nuclear Power Prototype
USN Electrician's Mate "A" School

CLIFFORD EVANS
46 Wright Lane
Des Moines, Iowa 50311
(515) 555-3187

SUMMARY OF QUALIFICATIONS

Over fifteen years experience assisting in changing new launch lines into efficient production lines. Strengths include: supervision ability, comprehending machine setups, and writing guides and procedures to assist in the training of production workers.

WORK EXPERIENCE

1989-Present   **Porter Productions, Des Moines, IA**

                       Foreman

                       Supervise 25 people on a new production line that manufactures over 1,200 parts per shift. Assisted in writing of machine process procedures and quality control sheets for the plant production lines.

1984-1989   **Global Heat Exchange, Inc., Davenport, IA**

     1989   **General Foreman**

                       Managed the work force on the coil line which produced over 1,000 units per shift. Set up the production schedule and ordered materials for the assembly of evaporators and condensers.

   1984-1989   **Machine Setup**

                       Assisted in the launching of new copper/aluminum line. Wrote the standard operating procedures, troubleshooting guides, and machine setup procedures. Trained operators to set up and operate all machines.

Page 2

1966-1983	**Andersen Glass Works, Davenport, IA**

1973-1983   **Machine Setup**

Set up and troubleshot 20 grinding machines. Participated in the launching of a new funnel press line. Set up machinery in Korea and trained the Korean personnel for a new glass plant.

1971-1973   **Machine Maintenance**

Maintained the acid, polishing, grinding, and filtering systems for all cold end operations.

1966-1971   **Ware Handler**

Operated grinding machines.

EDUCATION

DeVry Institute of Technology
Courses included:
Basic Electronics
Fundamentals of Process Control
Basic Language I
Fundamentals of Computer and Basic Language

MILITARY

U.S. Army, 1966-1968
Honorable Discharge

Had supervision training.
Served in Korea for 15 months.

Russ Johnson

100 Cooper Road
Ithaca, NY 10004
(212) 555-4103

OVER 15 YEARS EXPERIENCE IN MANUFACTURING OPERATIONS WITH AN EMPHASIS ON CLASSICAL INDUSTRIAL ENGINEERING, PROCESS IMPROVEMENTS, COST REDUCTIONS, MANPOWER REDUCTIONS, IMPLEMENTATION OF ADVANCED AUTOMATED MANUFACTURING PROCESSES AND SYSTEMS, PROJECT MANAGEMENT, AND GENERAL FLOOR TROUBLESHOOTING.

Summary of Experience

Knight Glassware, Ithaca, NY   1982 - 1993

Senior Industrial Engineer

Responsible for spear-heading "state-of-the-art" fully automated finishing operations. Conducted manufacturing studies on departmental processes and methods to determine standards, process improvements, equipment evaluations, automation of test and assembly departments, introduction of robotics for material handling, and routings.

o   Designed, coordinated and implemented personal computing hardware and software technology for total division.

o   Administered Quality of Worklife program and facilitated data for major conference aimed at product quality improvement.

o   Coordinated facilities consolidation effort.

o   Initiated program to fully automate department operations.

-2-

John Deere Works, Des Moines, IA   **1974 - 1978**

Industrial Engineer

Gained experience in machining, quality control, supervision, tooling processes, and new product introduction.

o   Introduced preventive maintenance program for heavy machinery.

o   Improved methods of material handling and sub-assembly.

Education

Cornell University	1982	MBA, Operations and Systems Management
Purdue University	1979	B.S., Mechanical Engineering

Memberships/Associations

Industrial Engineering Society
National Black MBA Association

References

Furnished upon request.

TOM HEALEY
606 WINSTON WAY
RALEIGH, NC 27706
(919) 555-3218

EDUCATION

MBA, Duke University - 1986
BS, Mechanical Engineering, University of North Carolina - 1970

SUMMARY OF EMPLOYMENT

Manufacturing engineer and production manager with twenty-three years experience. Recent experiences are in JIT and focused factories. Demonstrated strengths in leading a manufacturing organization in support of an aggressive corporate strategy.

EMPLOYMENT

May 1979 to Present   Raleigh Technology Group, Raleigh, NC

Jan 90 - Present   **Engineering and Production Manager**

Planned, directed, and controlled the definition, development and implementation of a large scale new manufacturing venture.
** Directed the definition and development of an engineer-to-order job shop.
** Provided executive leadership for the planning, organization, and selection of the business systems that supported the production shop.

Sept 87 - Jan 90   **Engineering and Production Manager**

Planned, directed, organized, and controlled the introduction of a new technology computer keyboard into manufacture. The resultant production facility was a high volume, progressive assembly shop utilizing Just-In-Time principles and Total Quality Control concepts.
** Directed the definition of the JIT manufacturing process and managed the development of robotics and hard automation process equipment.
** Planned and directed the implementation of a materials requirement planning system that supported a volatile product demand.
** Planned, developed, and implemented a unique quality control plan with vendors.

Jan 87 - Sept 87   **Engineering Manager, Process**

Organized, planned, and directed the development of a re-engineered metal working operation.
** Managed the turnaround of a troubled metal working operation into JIT cells.

TOM HEALEY

May 79 - Jan 87	<u>Engineering Manager, Facilities</u>

Planned, organized, directed, and controlled the transition of a metal working, mechanical assembly factory into a circuit card and light mechanical assembly factory.
** Directed and managed the turnaround of a large facilities engineering group by implementing a PERT-based management system.
** Planned, organized, and managed the re-engineering of a metal working factory to focused factories utilizing JIT principles.

May 70 - May 79   Eastern Technological Systems, Charlotte, NC

Sept 78 - May 79   <u>Production Supervisor</u>

Planned and managed production of telephone dials in a high volume, low option production shop.

May 70 - Sept 78   <u>Facilities Project Engineer</u>

Engineered, planned, organized, and controlled facilities construction projects. Responsible for the design, budgeting, and contract administration for new facilities projects.

<u>PROFESSIONAL ACCREDITATION</u>

Registered Professional Engineer - North Carolina
APICS Certified in Production and Inventory Management

Lawrence Ho

46 95th Street S.
Rockford, IL 61108
(815) 555-6632

EMPLOYMENT

1979 - Present CATERPILLAR COMPONENT WORKS
Rockford, Illinois

Project/Chemical Paint Engineer

Initially responsible for the works start up and support paint systems including: anodic electrocoat, cathodic electrocoat, conventional air, airless, electrostatic air, 3 and 5 stage iron phosphate pre-treatment, and deionized water units. After start up, responsible for systems and involved with zinc phosphate, manganese phosphate, and plating.

Special projects involving new materials or technologies included: water-reducible high solids, compliance stripping, compliance paint booth.

1976 - 1979 ROCKFORD INDUSTRIES
Rockford, Illinois

Electrocoating Superintendent

Responsible for all aspects of paint and coating/finishing of tool boxes and roller cabinets. Redesigned product and system to improve reject rate. Trained shift supervisor and hourly operators in equipment usage and applications.

1975 - 1976 STEEL TANKS, INC.
Dixon, Illinois

Finishing Consultant

Manufacturer of bolted steel tanks. Responsible for specifying methods and equipment, scheduling maintenance, and supervising paint room personnel. Successfully solved problems relating to the application of critical engineered finishes to resist oilfield, chemical, dry food, and potable water storage.
Travelled extensively in Europe
Enjoy painting, water polo, and tennis

1973 - 1975 ILLINOIS DOOR COMPANY
Peoria, Illinois

Finishing Manager

Manufacturer of metal closets and entry doors. Supervised building construction, layout, and equipment installation. Operated and maintained electrocoat and automatic reciprocating electrostatic air spray systems. Responsible for plant start up and the training of personnel.

1964 - 1973 PEORIA PRODUCTS
Peoria, Illinois

Finishing Engineer

Responsible for all equipment, applications, layout, automation systems and process improvements for paint, plating, and silk screen. Acted as liaison between product engineering, testing, and suppliers/vendors to assure quality and manufacturability.

EDUCATION

BS Industrial Engineering
Rockford College, 1959

5 years as electronic technician, U.S.A.F.

CURRICULUM VITAE

Horst Von Neumann

12369 Lake Drive
Philadelphia, PA 19104
(215) 555-9851

EDUCATION:

MS Electrical Engineering
Technical University of Munich, 1973

PhD Solid State Physics, Electronics
Technical University of Munich, 1980

EMPLOYMENT:

1990 to Present

Transformers, Inc., Philadelphia, PA

New Products Sales Manager

Organized a new sales department for a $30 million company specializing in servicing of electric transformers. Hired additional salespeople. Opened up a new sales office in Indiana. Prepared a sales plan for the disposal of PCB transformers.

1989 to 1990

Tri-State Industrial Sealants, Pittsburgh, PA

Marketing Manager

Co-wrote a strategic plan outlining marketing/selling/servicing aspects of the market resulting in a major reorganization of the Automotive Business Group. Managed product line, directed development of new products, set prices, and worked directly with the automotive companies in Detroit.

1988 to 1989	Carnegie Welding Group, Pittsburgh, PA

Engineer, Project Coordinator

Prepared a study of competitive machines which prompted company management to introduce a family of small welders, instead of only one, as originally planned. Acted as project coordinator for a welder with the task of speeding up market introduction of the machine. Helped to shorten the implementation schedule by 9 weeks.

1982 to 1988	Mellon Manufacturers Group, Philadelphia, PA
1985 to 1988	International Sales Director

Managed international sales for this $50 million manufacturer of industrial food processing equipment. Doubled volume of export sales from 1985 to 1987. Prepared and implemented a sales plan for Europe, stressing support for local markets. Established close contact with the Japanese distributor and Japanese customers. Led development of a new product line aimed at overseas food processors reversing sales decline in this market.

1982 to 1985	Sales Engineer

Sold food processing equipment to domestic and overseas accounts.

1980 to 1981	Bonn Engineering, Bonn, Germany

Design Engineer

Worked in the electrical engineering group for this company involved in sewage treatment plant design. Designed power distribution and controls.

1973 to 1980	University of Munich, Munich Germany
	Assistant Professor
	Involved in research and teaching. Directed research projects on aging phenomena in electronic insulating materials. Wrote and co-wrote 10 papers and reports on this subject. Lectured on high voltage insulation, theory of electricity, and dielectric measurement techniques.
PERSONAL:	Speak fluent German, French, and Spanish Naturalized U.S. citizen Married, two children
REFERENCES:	Furnished on request.

EMILIO LOPEZ

4638 Via Veracruz
Galveston, TX 77333
(409) 555-6418

OBJECTIVE:	To secure employment which will best utilize my twenty years experience as a construction project manager and which will correspond with my overall career goals.
EXPERIENCE: 6/90 to Present	YUMA ASSOCIATES Galveston, TX <u>Estimator</u> Produce bid proposals for bridge and water-main construction.
1988 to 1990	S.J. ANDREWS CONSTRUCTION Dallas, TX <u>Project Manager/Estimator</u> Bid sewer, water, storm drains for municipalities in Dallas and surrounding areas. Also performed as project manager for some projects.
1986 to 1988	FREEMAN DEVELOPMENT Dallas, TX <u>Construction Project Manager</u> Responsible for field supervision for various projects including water lines, sewer projects, concrete bank protection, site preparation, and asphalt replacement. Also maintained quality control, estimated, and bid contracts.
1983 to 1986	LOPEZ AND PALMA CONSTRUCTION Lubbock, TX <u>President/Co-owner</u> Duties included estimating, management, and field supervision of 40 employees. Projects were primarily underground utilities, electrical, and asphaltic concrete replacement for various private developers and the city of Lubbock.

1981 to 1983   WILLINGHAM INTERNATIONAL
                       Chiang Mai, Thailand
                       <u>General Superintendent</u>
                       Supervised 13 superintendents and 1500
                       craft workers in a refinery. In charge
                       of installation of pumps, valves, pipe
                       racks, entire tank farm, and steel
                       lines.

1980 to 1981   BANK OF AMERICA
                       Singapore
                       <u>Highway Engineer</u>
                       Completed 1-year contract on a technical
                       assistance team to study development of
                       Singapore domestic construction
                       industry. Duties included selection of
                       criteria for implementing appropriate
                       project demonstration sites for roads,
                       irrigation, and housing. Assigned as
                       field monitor to provide direct
                       assistance to domestic contractors
                       performing work. Identified major
                       constraints to progress and offered
                       recommendations to clear or minimize
                       constraints.

1978 to 1980   MADRIGAL ENGINEERS
                       San Antonio, TX
                       <u>Project Manager</u>
                       Supervised construction of 20-story high
                       rise. Duties included all men,
                       subcontractors, and materials for
                       completion of project.

                       Mexico
                       <u>Project Manager</u>
                       Responsible for all men, equipment, and
                       material for widening of the Blanco
                       River. Work included secondary roads,
                       cofferdams, mass excavations, and
                       concrete retaining walls.

LOPEZ   **PAGE 3**

1976 to 1978   WILLINGHAM INTERNATIONAL
                      Egypt
                      General Superintendent
                      General Superintendent on gas gathering
                      facility. Responsible for construction
                      involving placing concrete for all pip
                      rack foundations, pipeways, and
                      highways.

1973 to 1976   DESERT POWER CORPORATION
                      Phoenix, AZ
                      Area Superintendent

                      Coordinated all crafts in construction
                      of control room on nuclear power plant.
                      Ironworker Superintendent in charge of
                      350 ironworkers for construction of
                      turbines.

1969 to 1973   OKLAHOMA PROPERTIES, INC.
                      Tulsa, OK
                      Project Manager
                      Supervised office personnel and
                      construction of luxury apartment
                      complex. In charge of negotiations,
                      subcontractors, and bidding/estimating.
                      Supervised engineers and architects and
                      plans for a 18-story downtown building.
                      Responsible for al subcontract materials
                      and crafts to construct the high-rise.
                      Supervised all subcontractors and
                      engineers in the planning and
                      construction of 10-story cast in place
                      concrete building.

EDUCATION: B.S. CIVIL ENGINEERING
                      Texas A&M University/College Station

REFERENCES: Available upon request.

Marjorie Macon Long

CURRENT ADDRESS
460 East Butte Lane
Denver, CO 80208
Phone: 303-555-6423

OBJECTIVE   To secure a position which utilizes my skills and talents.

EDUCATION   University of Colorado, Boulder, CO
                 Master of Business Administration, 1983
                 Organizational Development

                 Mesa College, Grand Junction, CO
                 Bachelor of Science, 1977
                 Health, Physical Education, and Recreation

EXPERIENCE   Material Control Analyst   12/83 - Present
                 Colorado Electronics and Refrigeration Corporation
                 Denver, CO

                 -    Scheduled five final assembly lines and three sub-assembly
                      lines for fuel senders and pump senders
                 -    Order and input computer transactions for vendors
                 -    Develop organizational material to improve time management
                      in department
                 -    Cross-trained in traffic analyst position
                 -    Coordinate shipments with body and assembly plants
                 -    Reconcile inventory transactions
                 -    Responsible for disposition of rejected material

                 Quality Control Supervisor   6/82 - 11/83
                 American Container
                 Denver, CO

                 -    Developed quality grid management programs
                 -    Supervised all management and hourly employees in quality
                      programs
                 -    Administered and directed all special projects for cost savings

- Reorganized and developed cross-training procedures of office personnel
- Developed forecasting reports for raw material usage
- Directed and administered customer plant tours

Planning Supervisor   2/82 - 6/82
American Container
Denver, CO

- Supervised corrugator scheduler
- Supervised Quality Control programs
- Established statistical analysis of raw material usage

Production Management Trainee   6/81 - 2/82
American Container
Denver, CO

- Participated in Management Training programs
- Research Assistant in marketing survey
- Production training in finishing and printing departments
- Supervised three employees
- Assisted in drafting capital appropriations

Scheduling Clerk   6/79 - 5/81
American Container
Denver, CO

- Scheduled corrugator and supporting operations
- Purchased raw materials
- Cross-trained in order entry and billing clerk positions
- Trained personnel in inventory control

Material Control Clerk   2/79 - 6/79
American Container
Salt Lake City, UT

- Processed inbound and outbound shipments
- Administrated employee insurance claims

3

Circulation Assistant Manager   5/77 - 2/79
Salt Lake City Tribune
Salt Lake City, UT

-       Supervised mailroom department
-       Supervised eight paper carriers
-       Assisted in rural delivery management

Part-time Work

-       Emergency Medical Technician - 1983 - 1985
-       Girls Gymnastics Coach - Northview High School - 1981
-       Highland Elementary Girls Basketball Coach - 1980
-       CHSAA Girls Athletic Official - 1973 - 1981

ACTIVITIES   Assisted in Special Olympics 1992
                 Member of American Red Cross
                 Member of American Business Women's Association

REFERENCES   Furnished on request.

MICHAEL COLLINS
381 East 81st, #27
New York, NY 10028
(212) 555-3953

Award winning Technical Educator and Computer Support Specialist which can make me an outstanding contributor to your organization in the areas of:

MANAGEMENT INFORMATION SYSTEMS
TECHNICAL EDUCATION
COMPUTER SYSTEMS SUPPORT

EDUCATION

U.S. NAVY ELECTRONIC TRAINING
1979-1982

SUBMARINER CERTIFICATION
1980

TRAINING AND EXPERTISE

Super Computer Integrated Systems
Mainframes through Micros
Peripheral Equipment
Personal Computer Applications

PERSONAL

Football referee in Collegiate League
Music - piano and trumpet

QUALIFICATIONS

TECHNICAL TRAINER - Achieved outstanding recognition as an educator. Selected and supervised staff of instructors.

CREATOR and DEVELOPER - Researched, created, packaged, and implemented training programs in areas of quality management, computer hardware, and computer software.

TECHNICAL WRITER - Wrote program manuals, self-taught programs, and on-the-job training manuals. Served as a resource to writing staffs.

COMPUTER SUPPORT SPECIALIST - Have comprehensive experience in computer hardware troubleshooting, repair of equipment, and maintenance of integrated systems.

CAREER SUMMARY

XEROX INTERNATIONAL
(1986-Present)

TRAINING SPECIALIST

- Create, develop, and conduct training for employees and customers in formal and informal settings.

- Evaluate courses to determine quality of content and format as well as recommend selection of appropriate staff trainers.

- Indirectly responsible for marketing training programs to international and domestic clients.

U.S. NAVY
(1978-1986)

COMPUTER SYSTEMS SUPPORT
Technical Trainer

- Responsible for training the theory and application of electronics to nontechnical personnel.

- Responsible for providing total systems maintenance support under all conditions for assigned duty aboard a roving missile submarine.

HERBERT RICE

28 Baker Street
Flint, MI 48506
(313) 555-4039

CAREER	Project/Application Engineer for a manufacturer implementing advanced automation systems.
EDUCATION	Michigan State University, East Lansing, Michigan Bachelor of Science, December 1984 Mechanical Engineering Technology Lawrence Institute of Technology, Southfield, Michigan Certificate in Management Program Basic Project Management
EXPERIENCE	Automation Engineering Specialist Honda Trucks, Flint, Michigan (3/89 - Present)

- Supervise skilled trades in the Body Shop
- Supervise electricians in the electronic repair crib
- Planned and directed the installation of spot welding robots on truck lines

Project/Design Engineer
Bell Laboratories, Detroit, Michigan
(3/87 - 3/89)

- Planned, scheduled, and controlled project resources
- Managed mechanical/electrical engineers and shop personnel during project life
- Specified and procured equipment from vendors
- Insured quality systems are built with minimal cost and time
- Estimated cost of equipment and labor

Advanced Manufacturing Engineer
Allison Transmission, Speedway, Indiana
(10/84 - 3/87)

- Introduced automation projects, special application machines, and tooling
- Resolved and determined corrective action for production problems involving automation systems
- Initiated and incorporated cost-saving ideas
- Oversaw acquisition of high volume assembly equipment
- Oversaw maintenance of industrial robots

AUTOMATION EQUIPMENT	**ROBOTIC SYSTEMS**

- Adept I, II, and III, Cincinnati Milacron hydraulic and electrical, GMF Robotics, Unimation

MACHINE VISION SYSTEMS

- Adept Technology – binary, greyscale, and robot guidance systems

COMPUTER AIDED DESIGN SYSTEMS

- Versacad

COMPUTER SOFTWARE	Fortran, Pascal, Basic, PCtools, Formtool, WordPerfect
REFERENCES	Available upon request.

RESUME

CHARLES McVEY
52 Elm Street
Grand Rapids, MI 49504
(616) 555-9610

OBJECTIVE

Process or Production Engineering Management position in a high-tech industrial or automotive finishing industry.

WORK EXPERIENCE

Fischer Industries, Grand Rapids, MI   6/88 - Present

Senior Finishing Engineer

Responsibilities include the supervision and coordination of major capital finishing and facilities projects at four manufacturing plants. Heavy emphasis is placed on implementing new paint application processes including: robotic system integration, PLC controls and devices, electrostatic painting equipment, washers, spraybooths, and chemicals. Extensive work was done implementing BC/CC, powder, 2K, HSE, and waterborne and UV coating technologies on metal, plastic, and wood.

McDonald Automotive Works, East Lansing, MI   1/84 - 5/88

Research Engineer (2/85 - 5/88)

Provided in-plant process engineering support and start-up assistance involving facilities, circulations systems, pneumatic, electrical and fluid controls, robotics, and electrostatic application equipment to major automobile manufacturers. Also provided process input and start-up assistance for fascia painting facility.

Page 2

Application Engineer (1/84 - 2/85)

Provided in-plant engineering and application expertise to automotive manufacturers during design and start-up in support of OEM coatings sales. Worked extensively in modular base coat/clear coat and high solid enamel systems.

Automotive Technology, Inc., East Lansing, MI   3/79 - 1/84

Regional Distribution Supervisor (3/83 - 1/84)

Supervised the sales efforts of company's distributor network in the automotive industry in Canada, the U.S., and Mexico.

Manager of Training (8/81 - 12/82)

Wrote, produced, and directed 10 videotapes used in the training of internal supervisory, engineering, and field service personnel. Developed a sales training program for the company's distributor network. Conducted seminars for large groups of customers.

Service Engineer (3/79 - 9/79)

Installed and serviced large industrial electrostatic painting systems.

EDUCATION

Master of Science Degree, Industrial Education Technology
Health and Safety Minor, May 1979
Michigan State University

Bachelor of Science Degree, Industrial Education Technology
Health and Safety Minor, July 1975
GMI Engineering & Management Institute

RESUME

Leroy Anderson
P.O. Box 1145
Golden, Colorado 80401
(303) 555-3221

EDUCATION

UNIVERSITY:	California Institute of Technology Pasadena, CA B.S. Mining Engineering - 1957 B.S. Geological Engineering - 1958
PROFESSIONAL AWARDS:	American Institute of Mining & Metallurgy Proficiency Medal, 1988 Regional Representative, Prospectors & Developers Association of America

EXPERIENCE

I have worked with Precambrian Shield and sedimentary rocks in Eastern Canada, Saudi Arabia, Thailand, United States, Brazil, Guyana, and Costa Rica in search of various industrial minerals, non-metallics, salt-potash, bauxite, iron, base metals, precious metals, uranium, graphite, tar sands, oil shales, and coal. I have over thirty years of exploration experience ranging from the Eastern Arctic to the Amazon River and the Middle East.

The early stages of my career were confined to short-term employment contracts in remote areas. Then ten years were spent with two major companies supervising geochemical, geophysical, geologic, photo interpretation, and diamond drilling programs. Also, my experience has extended into underground geological drilling and open pit operations. During this period I gained a working knowledge of French and Portuguese.

Page 2

Presently, I am maintaining a small, well-equipped office in downtown Golden, Colorado, which specializes in long- or short-term contracts, either domestic or foreign. The clientele ranges from large multinational mining companies to junior mining companies, promoters, and prospectors. The work includes examining/evaluating properties for Qualifying Reports to Investment Reports on properties that contain mills and underground workings of producers or past producers. Another phase of work or service is outlining and supervising administration, which ranges from initiating large "grass root" exploration programs to detailed drilling of developed mineral deposits. During this course of work, I integrate and correlate numerous other consulting services such as directional drilling, mud, cement, casing, downhole testing, and geophysics. To facilitate this work, I organize and maintain staking, linecutting, geochemical, and geophysical surveys.

PREVIOUS EMPLOYMENT

Geological Exploration Consulting	December 1973 - Present Providing consulting services to over 75 clients during the last 20 years.
Ford Corporation of Canada	January 1968 - November 1973 Resident Exploration Geologist Atlantic Provinces, Quebec, Costa Rica
Columbia Bauxite Co.	January 1967 - January 1968 Geologist Guyana
Aluminum Company, Ltd.	August 1965 - January 1967 Exploration Geologist Amazon River, Brazil
Ford Corporation of Canada	January 1962 - August 1965 Project Geologist Nova Scotia, New Brunswick

Page 3

W.B. Stone Engineering   May 1961 - January 1962
Field Geologist & Supervisor
of Underground Development
Drilling
Newfoundland, Ontario, Quebec

Mining Corp. of Alaska   January 1961 - May 1961
Asst. Geophysical Operator
Juneau, Alaska

Little Long Uranium Mines   May 1960 - January 1961
Field Geologist
Fort Hope, Ontario, Quebec

Century Mines Ltd.   May 1959 - October 1960
Field Geologist
Quebec and Ontario

U.S. Army Corps of Engineers   June 1958 - May 1959
San Francisco, California

Mid-Quebec Mines Ltd.   1957 - Ungava, Quebec (summer
employment)

Canadian Minerals Ltd.   1956 - Lac Albanel, Quebec
(summer employment)

CHARLES SANFORD
12 MOBILE DRIVE
BIRMINGHAM, AL 35230
(205) 555-4986

OVERVIEW

An experienced, creative, and results-oriented Project Engineer/Manager with a demonstrated ability to assume major responsibilities and the technical and managerial skills required to "make it happen." Expertise in evaluating product designs, analyzing production systems, and conceiving, developing, and directing the implementation of solutions to enhance productivity and improve operational productivity. I understand the importance of teamwork as well as competent and reliable individual performance. Desire a "take charge" position that will stimulate professional and personal growth and encourage individual initiative and creativity.

WORK EXPERIENCE

United Technologies, Inc., Birmingham, AL

July 1989 - Present:	Supervisor, Producibility Engineering Group
April 1989 - June 1989:	Industrial Engineer

Accomplishments:

- Established and developed a new functional group, Producibility Engineering, within Operations. Responsible for ensuring low cost manufacturability of product designs and improving the productivity of production operations.

- Directed and conducted new product design evaluations and analyses which resulted in the recommendation and acceptance of design improvements representing over $5 million dollars in production cost avoidance on current contracts and permitted more competitive pricing on proposals for future business.

- Developed format and procedure and directed construction of a comprehensive and detailed process flow chart of factory operations which was analyzed to identify major opportunities for improvement and facilitated rational deployment of resources to increase efficiency of operations.

- Conceived, developed, and coordinated the implementation of a JIT/Kanban (pull) production control system which reduced associated WIP inventory levels.

- Launched a part standardization program with pilot project.

Page 2

World Communications, Inc., Nashville, TN

November 1985 - March 1989:   Manufacturing Research Engineer
January 1985 - October 1985:   Associate Manufacturing Research Engineer

Accomplishments:

- Conceived, developed, and implemented an automated manufacturing system.

- Conceived, validated technical feasibility, priced, scheduled, and prepared a detailed technical and financial proposal for the development of an automated machining and assembly system to reduce platform fabrication cost.

- Coordinated an assessment of automated manufacturing system capabilities/limitations and prepared design guidelines for engineering to ensure that new product designs would be compatible with existing production resources.

- Created and administered a shop floor survey/interview program which identified and documented current production difficulties and recommendations for design improvements in preparation for a major government contract.

- Originated control documentation forms, established procedures, and administered the operations of producibility team which identified and proposed design solutions with reduced production cost impact.

EDUCATION

University of Tennessee, Knoxville, TN. School of Business Administration and Economics.
Master of Science in Business Administration degree expected in June.
Production and Management Systems Analysis.
GPA 4.0.

Auburn University, Auburn, AL.
Bachelor of Mechanical Engineering, 1984.
GPA 3.8.

ACHIEVEMENTS AND AWARDS

- Truth Linkage Competition Design Award, for cam linkage design, 1984.

- World Communications, Inc. "Award of Achievement," for contributions to method improvement/cost reduction program, 1986.

- World Communications, Inc. "Product Excellence Awards," for dedication to quality workmanship and product improvement, 1987.

MEMBERSHIPS

- Society of Manufacturing Engineers

- Robotics International

- Institute of Industrial Engineers

REFERENCES AVAILABLE UPON REQUEST.

ARNOLD BYERS
480 HELENA DRIVE
BILLINGS, MT 59101
(406) 555-4981

EXECUTIVE PROFILE

Experience

Mr. Byers has over 15 years of experience in the environmental field. Much of his experience has been in dealing with environmental matters throughout the United States.

He presently serves as Litigation and Environmental Claim Director for the Western Insurance Company. In that position, he directs the investigations of CERCLA, RCRA, LUST, and other types of environmental claims at local plant sites and at major Superfund sites. He manages complex environmental litigation and administrative law actions in all parts of the country.

Mr. Byers has also had government and other private sector experience in the environmental area. This latter experience includes being an attorney in private practice and a corporate attorney handling environmental compliance and general corporate legal matters for United Coal Company. At United, he served in several management positions including Director of Regulatory Affairs and Vice-President of Public and Governmental Affairs.

His experience in government includes being Deputy Director and Counsel to the Montana Office of Energy Policy. In addition to providing legal counsel to the agency, he also oversaw the agency's grant program for asbestos removal for schools and hospitals and had supervisory responsibilities for the agency's engineer's office and its technical services programs.

Publications

"OSM Regulations Affecting Old Mines," *Montana Mining Journal*, September, 1980
"OSM Surface Mining Regulations," Mineral Bureau Spring Workshop, Chicago, Illinois, April, 1982
"MSRTA Enforcement Hearing Planning and Strategy," Montana Continuing Legal Education Forum, November, 1989

Education

B.S., J.D., Ohio State University. Continuing legal education courses in environmental law, contracts, real estate, and civil litigation.

Licensure

State of Montana - Attorney No. 5555 55
State of North Dakota - Attorney No. 55555

Arnold Byers - 2

EXPERIENCE

Environmental Investigations

- Due diligence review for real estate transfers

- Environmental risk assessment

- Environmental audits for proposed acquisitions

- Third-party adjudication of cleanup costs for Superfund and other multiple party sites

- Environmental compliance audits

- Evaluation and analysis of insurance claims

Litigation Support Services

- Prepared expert witnesses to testify in environmental lawsuits

- Data research and interpretation

- Identification of other potentially responsible parties

- Computerized management of environmental data

DONALD McKINLEY

281 River Road ● *Sacramento, CA* ● *(916) 555-4783*

QUALIFIED BY: Thirty years experience concentrating on project prospecting, sales, feasibility, analysis, proposal and EPA permit preparation, contract negotiating, and engineering design.

EDUCATION: B.S.   Mechanical Engineering
University of Santa Clara, 1958

M.B.A.   Marketing and Production
University of Michigan, 1962

EXPERIENCE:

SOLID WASTE
PROCESSING: VICE-PRESIDENT, PROJECT DEVELOPMENT
CGA Systems
Sacramento, CA
1988 - Present

Facility design, proposals, specs, and EPA permit writing.

COGENERATION: PROJECT ANALYST
Griswald Engineering
Sacramento, CA
1986 - 1988

Steam generation, gas turbines, and large diesel generators.

HVAC DESIGN: CONSULTING ENGINEER
Apple, Ellis Technologies
Sacramento, CA
1984 - 1986

Manufacturing and office retrofit.

-2-

HIGH SCHOOL
  MATHEMATICS: TEACHER
                      Reno High School
                      Reno, NV
                      1981 - 1984

                      Engineering Drawing and Industrial
                      Arts.

FUEL PURCHASE: FUEL CONTROL ADMINISTRATOR
                      Bay Maritime
                      San Diego, CA
                      1980

                      Worldwide fuel purchasing.

OIL TRADING: VICE-PRESIDENT, MARKETING
                      L.T. Cravens, Inc.
                      Seattle, WA
                      1978 - 1979

                      Alaskan crude oil, project
                      analysis, and raised venture
                      capital.

HVAC DESIGN: CONSULTING ENGINEER
                      Smith, Withers, & Associates
                      Seattle, WA
                      1976 - 1977

INDUSTRIAL
  REAL ESTATE: MANAGER
                      Prudential
                      Seattle, WA
                      1969 - 1975

                      Build-to-suit projects, sales,
                      leasing, and property development.

OTHER:
          Contract Manager, Nuclear Reactors, General
          Electric, 1969
          Systems Analyst, Quality Control, Babcock
          Engineering, 1966 - 1968
          Salesman, Industrial HVAC, The York Co., 1962
          - 1966

-3-

RESUME SUPPLEMENT:

SOLID WASTE:

1988 - Present: CGA Systems.
Prepared three complete project-winning proposals under competitive conditions. The three projects use state-of-the-art technology of central-station recycling, interior MSW composting, and sludge co-composting capabilities. Each incorporates a custom-designed innovative system approach and unique application of a variety of general and proprietary machinery.

In mid-1989, prepared a proposal for one of the largest recycling and front-end material preparation projects in the country. CGA systems was awarded the contract. Upon completion in 1994, the system will be the most sophisticated and environmentally sound recycling center for pre-incineration preparation of MSW of any facility in the country.

HVAC:

1986 - 1987: Griswald Engineering.
HVAC design and drafting of newspaper printing plant. Co-generation project analysis.

1986: Apple Corporation.
One of two engineers handling HVAC problems of 10 manufacturing and office buildings. Retrofitted computer chip manufacturing facilities.

1984 - 1985: Ellis Technologies.
Retrofit design and drafting for computer chip manufacturing building. Clean room retrofit.

HVAC design and drafting. Retrofit General Motors assembly plant. Building was being converted to rocket production for U.S.A.F.

Gloria Rapp
20 Mayfair Boulevard, #10
Burlington, VT 05401
802-555-3378

OBJECTIVE: TO GAIN AN ENTRY LEVEL POSITION IN SOFTWARE DEVELOPMENT FOR MICROCOMPUTERS.

EDUCATION: UNIVERSITY OF VERMONT, BURLINGTON, VT
Pursuing a bachelor's degree in Computer Science. Course work includes computer science, mathematics (honors sequence of calculus, linear algebra, differential equations, and modern algebra) and classes in logic and operations research, physics, engineering, and linguistics. Graduation date: May 1994.

EXPERIENCE:

9/90 - Present   Residential Computer Coordinator, University of Vermont
Work with residence staff to integrate electronic information resources into residential education agenda. Customize and support educational software. Hold small class/seminars on topics of special interest for residents.

7/93 - 9/93   Lecturer, Middlebury College, Middlebury, VT
Taught a basic computer course. This summer class introduced the basic techniques for using the Macintosh computer to gifted high school students with little or no computing exposure.

7/92 - 9/92   Software Consultant, New Age Computer Co., Montpelier, VT
Wrote a technical reference manual and a users guide for existing vehicle maintenance database. Modified existing code to allow integration of external utilities with the system. Created utilities to expunge outdated information, export information in a general form to external software packages, and allow users to create generic templates to generate reports of often-repeated analysis.

ADDITIONAL INFORMATION:

* Member, Women Software Engineers
* Enjoy skiing, running, and volleyball
* Fluent in German

FRED STEVENS

Present Address
86 College Lane, #5
Princeton, NJ 08544
(609) 555-3061

Permanent Address
18602 Mann Drive
Tarreytown, NY 10591
(914) 555-3440

OBJECTIVE   Full-time position in telecommunications
research and development, particularly in
optical fiber networks, satellite
communication, or antenna design.

EDUCATION   Princeton University
Currently pursuing Masters of Science in
Electrical Engineering with a concentration
in telecommunications and fiber optics.
Expected Graduation: June 1994

Massachusetts Institute of Technology
Bachelor of Science with Highest Distinction
in Electrical Engineering, May 1991.

EXPERIENCE   Connecticut Pipe Company, Bridgeport, CT
Summer 1992

SENIOR STAFF TECHNOLOGIST: Conducted
research on optical fiber communications
systems.   Primary research was an
experimental study of privacy and security
issues in passive, fiber-to-the-home
networks.

Princeton University, Department of
Electrical Engineering
1991-1993

TEACHING ASSISTANT: Controls Courses and
Introduction to Electronics Laboratory.

Gulf Oil, Houston, TX
Summer 1991

SPECIAL TECHNICAL ASSISTANT: Installed
hardware and software for computer control of
test equipment, conducted stress tests on
circuit boards, and wrote software to capture
and plot oscilloscope waveforms.

Katherine Fang
620 Bayview, Apt. 19
Hayward, CA 94542
(510) 555-6817

OBJECTIVE   A position in research and development in the fields of thin film technologies, such as magnetic thin film technologies. Possibility for move into management preferred.

EDUCATION   University of California/Berkeley, Berkeley, CA
M.S., Materials Science and Engineering
Awarded 1990

The Claremont Colleges/Harvey Mudd College, Claremont, CA
B.S., Ceramic Engineering
Awarded 1987 with Great Distinction

EXPERIENCE

6/90-PRESENT   University of California/Berkeley, Berkeley, CA, Department of Materials Science and Engineering
Involved in design and building of a sputtering chamber.

6/87-6/90   The Claremont Colleges/Harvey Mudd College, Claremont, CA, Department of Ceramic Engineering
Researched properties of monolayer and multilayer films of alkanoic acids and alkylsiloxanes on solid surfaces.

ADDITIONAL
INFORMATION   Computer Languages: Basic, Fortran

Foreign Language: Chinese

Member:
* Materials Science & Engineering Association
* Inroads Academic Achievement Award
* Society of Women Engineers

Evan Lindquist
6189 Beach Road, #9C
Jacksonville, FL 32209

Home: (904) 555-1263   Work: (904) 555-4812

OBJECTIVE: To find a challenging position in the aerospace
                  industry which would utilize my highly specialized
                  engineering skills.

EDUCATION: Purdue University, West Lafayette, IN
                  Degree: B.S. in Aerospace Engineering, 1985

EXPERIENCE: Aerospace International, Jacksonville, FL

Jan. 88 to
Present   Title: Strength Engineer

                  Responsible for detailed stress analysis for engine
                  components. Hand and finite element methods were
                  utilized to examine the structural adequacy of various
                  components of the fan and core thrust reversers, the
                  composite inlet and accessory compartment doors, and
                  the fixed fan duct. Analysis included static,
                  thermal, and pressure loads in conformance with
                  military standards. Interfaced closely with the
                  design group during the preliminary release phase to
                  accelerate and optimize drawings.

June 87 to
Jan. 88   Aircraft Technology Corporation, Titusville, FL

                  Title: Value Engineer

                  Assigned to a training program to interface with
                  manufacturing. Goal of the project was to discover
                  fabrication techniques and difficulties and to improve
                  channels of communications between engineers and
                  manufacturing personnel. Concepts of value
                  engineering were used on selected intensive and
                  repeating problems. The project chosen was the air-
                  conditioning system for mid-size commercial aircraft.
                  Cost savings realized though this program were
                  considerable.

May 85 to
May 87   Goddard Aerospace Systems, Cocoa Beach, FL

                  Title: Stress Engineer

                  Responsible for engineering, analysis, and structural
                  substantiation on modifications for various commercial
                  aircraft. Worked closely with FAA Designated Engineer
                  Reps in design support work.

COMPUTER
EXPERIENCE: FEM programs such as NASTRAN, PATRAN, and PIPELINE on
                  both VAX and IBM.

<u>Resume</u>
Rachel L. Miller
4680 Campus Drive, #13C
Evanston, IL 60043
(708) 555-4917

OBJECTIVE

To obtain a position as editor or technical editor with a book, periodical, or newsletter computer publication.

EXPERIENCE
1987-Present

Professional Computer Books, Chicago, IL
Senior Editor of software information
Focus on review of new software products.

1986-1987

VCR Review, Sunnyvale, CA
Senior Editor of VCR facts manuals
Technical service data for the repair of Video Cassette Recorders by electronic technician.

1983-1986

Popular Electronics, Santa Clara, CA
Senior Editor of Computer facts manuals
Technical service data for the repair of home and business microcomputers by electronic technicians. Integral part of product development and start-up team.

1981-1983

Television Reports Inc., Mountain View, CA
Assistant Editor of Quickfacts manuals.
Quick reference television service manuals carried by electronic technicians in the field.

1979-1981

The Technician's Journal, Lincoln, NE
Compilation Editor Counter facts documentation
Cross-referenced listing of individual major component to replacement parts manufacturer's equivalent part. Eight major category divisions.

EDUCATION

University of Nebraska, Lincoln, NE
B.S. degree in Computer Technology, 1979

MARY PUGH   November, 1993

Present Address: 12 Palm Drive   (702) 555-6814
                      Las Vegas, NV 89154

Permanent Address: 238 Mountain Drive   (702) 555-4139
                      Reno, NV 89557

Objective: To obtain a position in information
                      systems, software development, or
                      related areas.

Education: University of Nevada/Las Vegas 9/89-6/93
                      B.S., Computer Science
                      G.P.A. 3.7/4.0

Experience: Summer 1992
                      Gulf Oil Co., Corpus Christi, TX
                      Computing Applications Intern Converted
                      right of way and claims database from
                      hierarchical structure to relational
                      structure in Database II and developed
                      its user interface. Required gaining
                      familiarity with Cobol DB3, PL/I, and
                      SQL, database design, and written and
                      oral presentations.

                      Summer 1991
                      Gulf Oil Co., Corpus Christi, TX
                      Subsurface Engineering Intern Conducted
                      research to evaluate the nature of
                      tubing leaks in gas lift valve and
                      flowing wells in southeast Texas and
                      developed recommendations to reduce
                      their occurrence. Involved in research
                      project design, use of Statistical
                      Analysis System, and written and oral
                      presentations.

Additional
Information: Knowledge of Ada, Basic, C, C++, DB2,
                      Pascal, SQL, Prolog, Smalltalk TSO and
                      UNIX operating system, Lotus 1-2-3.
                      Editor - Environmental Newsletter,
                      University of Nevada.
                      Member - University of Nevada Society of
                      Women in Engineering and Science.

Jane MacFarland

Current Address: Permanent Address:
P.O. Box 894   1211 Alfred Street
New Brunswick, NJ 08903   Newark, NJ 07102
(201) 555-4613   (201) 555-2809

OBJECTIVE

To obtain a position in the field of product design emphasizing product development or improvement and utilizing illustration, model-making, and other related skills.

EDUCATION

Rutgers/College of Engineering, New Brunswick, NJ
B.S. Mechanical Engineering, June 1993

Rutgers/College of Arts and Sciences, Camden, NJ
B.A. Psychology, June 1992

RELEVANT COURSEWORK

Calculus and Differential Equations
Physics
Materials Science
Stress Analysis
Software Engineering
Technology and Aesthetics
Electronics
Industrial Design
Manufacturing and Design
Marker Rendering and Mechanical Drawing

EXPERIENCE

Whirlpool Corporation
Manufacturing Engineer
June 1992 - September 1992
Amana, Iowa

Provided technical support to electronics section. Designed tools for use in semirigid and flexible cable manufacturing area. Developed plans for implementation of the purchased capital equipment and determined operating procedures for equipment.

General Electric Company
Production Controller
July 1990 - September 1991
Rochester, New York

Worked in product engineering and manufacturing section as an assistant planner. Distributed electrical kits to workers for assembly. Verified parts lists from engineering drawings. Used Lotus 1-2-3 to track daily status of project subassemblies.

Rutgers University Bookstore
Freelance Designer
September 1990 - September 1991
Camden, New Jersey

Produced graphic art by hand and computer-aided for dormitories, student groups, and other organizations. Used MacIntosh graphics programs to produce pins and shirts.

ADDITIONAL INFORMATION

Fluent in German

Teaching Assistant, Calculus, Rutgers/College of Engineering, 1993

Member, Society of Women Engineers

NAME: Jack Olsen

**PRESENT
ADDRESS:**   P.O. Box 4680   **TELEPHONE:**
              Cambridge, MA 02139   (617) 555-4890

**PERMANENT
ADDRESS:**   1225 Bay Drive   **TELEPHONE:**
              Portland, ME 04112   (207) 555-4910

OBJECTIVE: To obtain a position in information systems, software design/development or related area utilizing computer programming language skills.

EDUCATION:
9/89-6/93   MASSACHUSETTS INSTITUTE OF TECHNOLOGY
              Cambridge, MA
              B.S., Computer Science

EXPERIENCE:
Summer 92   City of Boston, Boston, MA
              <u>Management Information Systems Intern</u>:
              Designed computer systems for the Engineering Department. Involved significant user interaction and operating systems knowledge. Worked on IBM PC AT's and XT's.

Summer 91   Bosk Opthamalics, Cambridge, MA
              <u>Laboratory Technician</u>: Compiled research on the efficacy of polyethylene fluorination in extending shelf life of ophthalmic products. Used the liquid chromatography system, system troubleshooting, statistical analysis, and written and oral reports.

Summer 90   Bosk Opthamalics, Cambridge, MA
              <u>Associate Laboratory Technician</u>:
              Experimented on the efficacy of production barrier resins in hindering water loss. Required experiment design, statistical analysis, and written report. Familiarized co-workers with computer applications.

**ADDITIONAL
INFORMATION:**   Knowledge of Ada, C, C++, Basic, Pascal
                  Member, Society of Black Scientists and Engineers

PROFESSIONAL RESUME

Lola Velasquez
129 Via Robles
Houston, TX 77074
(713) 555-3219

CAREER OBJECTIVE
Desire a position in nongame animal research.

EDUCATION
University of Florida
Major: Biology
Minor: Psychology

Gainesville, FL
May 1993

EXPERIENCE
Summer 1991 & 1992

Bureau of Land Management
Anchorage , AK

STUDENT CONSERVATION ASSOCIATION VOLUNTEER

* Stream Management
* Timber Management
* Bat Study
General: Seventy-five percent of activity was spent in remote areas with minimal supervision. Extensive use of topographical maps and aerial photographs were utilized.

ASSISTANT BIOLOGIST

* Fish Taxonomy, Electrofishing, Seining
* Glacier - Delineation, 1990
* Conducted Educational Tours of Glaciers

RELATED EXPERIENCE

1988 to
Present

During this period, I have spent much of may spare time in the outdoors. Some of my activities include: birdwatching, plant identification, hunting, fishing, studying animal behavior, insect collecting, and keeping field journals.

Chapter Six

SAMPLE COVER LETTERS

300 Lake Shore Drive, #22
Chicago, IL 60603

ENVIRON Management
300 Butterfield Road
Oak Brook, IL 60521

Dear Personnel Director:

I am seeking a position in your firm which utilizes my
training in the environmental field. I am eager to work for
a firm that is implementing the latest environmental
advancements.

I earned a Bachelor of Science degree in Environmental
Health Science from Indiana University. Through two paid
internships with county health departments, I have
participated in health and safety training, regulatory
compliance, and on-site inspections. In addition, I am an
experienced technical writer and am proficient with several
word processing programs. During college, I was a member of
several organizations including Sigma Alpha Epsilon
fraternity, Environmental Health Association, and the
Bicycling Club. I have developed leadership and team
working skills through my work and college experiences.

I would be delighted to meet with you at your convenience to
discuss career opportunities with your firm. I can be
contacted by telephone at (312) 555-8961.

Sincerely,

Lee King

Enclosure: Resume

JASON DEAN
320 EAST 83rd STREET, #32
NEW YORK, NY 10028
(212) 555-9085

Ms. Linda Appleton
Overseas Trading Co.
25 Sixth Avenue
New York, NY 10013

Dear Ms. Appleton:

I am writing concerning possible employment opportunities with your firm. In particular, I am looking for a senior MIS management position in a progressive international firm. By way of an introduction, I have enclosed my resume.

As an MIS professional, I have had over 15 years experience in developing large-scale commercial business systems. I possess a solid technical background in multi-language programming and system design with extensive user interfacing.

Furthermore, I have direct experience in designing and establishing a systems and programming organization for Deloitte & Touche to enhance the firm's internal business system. I would welcome the opportunity to assist in the enhancement of Overseas Trading Co.'s information systems.

I would appreciate an opportunity to discuss my background with you in greater detail. I will look forward to hearing from you.

Sincerely,

Jason Dean

Enclosure

Lloyd G. Prescott
58 Mahwah Drive
Newark, New Jersey 07430
(201) 555-5297

Mr. Sam Palmer
Personnel Director
Michigan Engineering
P.O. Box 250
Detroit, MI 48226

Dear Mr. Palmer:

The purpose of this letter is to ask for your firm's consideration of me for any available position as a Senior Industrial Engineer.

I have approximately 15 years experience in industrial engineering and manufacturing process engineering with an emphasis on cost and manpower reductions, general floor troubleshooting, automation, equipment justification, and line balancing.

After you have reviewed my resume, I would appreciate the opportunity to discuss with you any industrial engineering openings. Thank you for your time.

I look forward to your response.

Sincerely,

Lloyd G. Prescott

Bechtel
P.O. Box 600
San Francisco, CA 94105
Attn: Rita Long
       Director of Human Resources

Dear Ms. Long,

Presently, I am the Project Coordinator for the University of Arizona
Physical Plant. My responsibilities include managing construction
projects, estimating, surveying, and supervising jobs.

I am seeking a more demanding position with an international
construction firm. My goal is to advance into a construction management
position that is concerned with achieving environmental compatablity on
the projects undertaken.

Enclosed is my resume for your review. I look forward to hearing from
you soon about career opportunities at Bechtel.

Sincerely,

Karen Adams

1685 Mountain Drive
Tucson, AZ 85720
(602) 555-8960

Mr. Bill Johnson
Columbus Engineering
200 East 16th Street
Columbus, OH 43216

Dear Mr. Johnson:

I am interested in interviewing with you for an entry level Civil Engineering position.

Recently, I received my masters in Civil Engineering from Ohio State University. Furthermore, I passed the April 1993 Engineer in Training examination.

While my work experience has been primarily in the structural analysis and design of bridges, roadways, and sewer systems, I am willing to consider positions in other related areas.

I have enclosed my resume for your review and consideration. I would like to meet with you personally to discuss my qualifications. I will follow up this letter with a telephone call in a few days.

Sincerely,

Mark F. Fulton

78 Prairie Road
Columbus, OH 43216
(614) 555-3981

Enclosure

FRED STEVENS
86 COLLEGE LANE, #5
PRINCETON, NJ 08544
(609) 555-3061

Mr. Richard Fraser
Western Telecom
3200 Valley Way
Englewood, CO 80111

Dear Mr. Fraser:

I am writing to obtain further information regarding employment with your corporation in telecommunications research and development. Specifically, I am interested in pursuing a career in optical fiber networks, satellite communication, or antenna design.

I will be graduating from Princeton University with a master's degree in Electrical Engineering in June. My studies have been concentrated in telecommunications and fiber optics. In addition, my summer internship enabled me to conduct research on the privacy and security issues in passive, fiber-to-the-home networks.

A copy of my resume is enclosed for your evaluation. If you need further information, I will be pleased to provide you with the necessary materials.

I look forward to discussing with you soon career opportunities at Western Telecom. I may be reached at the above number. Thank you for your consideration.

Sincerely,

Fred Stevens

Enclosure

Commercial Design
3500 Meridian
Carmel, IN 46032

Dear Victor Lord:

    I am very interested in pursuing a designer draftsman position with Commercial Design. Enclosed is a copy of my resume for your review.

    Through my present employment with The Industrial Design Group Inc., I have refined my design and detail skills. My work with this firm entails design development of mechanical, electrical, and plumbing systems for major commercial projects. I have gained first-hand experience with developing the construction details for the engineering and architectural concepts as well as preparing the final bid documentation.

    I look forward to hearing from you soon to further discuss my qualifications.

Sincerely,

Paul J. Richards
3300 Westwood Drive
Cuyahoga Falls, OH 44221
(216) 555-6929

EVAN LINDQUIST

6189 Beach Road, #9C, Jacksonville, FL 32209
904/555-1263

Jack Fang
General Aeronautics
100 Canaveral Road
Daytona Beach, FL 32014

Dear Mr. Fang:

The following is in response to your advertisement in last Tuesday's <u>Miami Herald</u>. I am interested in the aerospace engineer position with your firm.

Currently, I am working as a Strength Engineer for Aerospace International, where I am responsible for conducting detailed stress analysis for aircraft engine components. Previously, I have been a Value Engineer with Aircraft Technology Corporation working on aircraft air conditioning systems and a Stress Engineer with Goddard Aerospace Systems working on various commercial aircraft. Based on my experience, I believe that I could make a valuable contribution to General Aeronautics.

I hope to further discuss my qualifications with you in an interview.

Yours Truly,

Evan Lindquist

enclosure

Joseph E. Hart
Human Resources
Carnegie Steel
325 Steel Road
Gary, IN 46408

Dear Mr. Hart:

I wish to apply for a position as an electrical engineer with Carnegie Steel. I possess a bachelor's and master's degree in electrical engineering. Also, I have worked for over 18 years as a steelmaking reliability supervisor and manager and as a steel operations maintenance engineer. This extensive experience coupled with my personal interest could be of value to your firm.

For your review, I am enclosing my resume. Please feel free to call me at (219) 555-6823 to set up an interview.

Sincerely Yours,

Scott Monroe
64 Fountain Lake Road
Gary, IN 46408

Enclosure

125 College Way
Princeton, NJ 08545
609-555-1304

Sandia Robotics
Human Resources
500 East 29th Street
Trenton, NJ 08391

Dear Sir/Madam:

I am writing to you with the hope that you might have an opening soon in your robotics laboratory for a programmer. If you do not, I would appreciate your keeping my resume on file for upcoming opportunities.

My course work for a bachelor's degree in Mechanical Engineering at Princeton University will be completed in May 1994. Currently, I am performing independent robotics research on the use of Linear-Motor-Robots in assembly as a result of my research fellowship.

People who know me well consider me to be dedicated, hard-working, and creative. I enjoy challenging work and perform well under pressure. I believe that these characteristics fit with the type of professional you would be seeking.

Thank you for considering my qualifications. I look forward to hearing from you soon.

Sincerely,

Rachel Schwartzman

Patricia Butterfield
1480 Dean Road
Sacramento, CA 95819

Ms. Consuela Flores
EnviroTek
33 Sierra Road
Los Angeles, CA 90024

Dear Ms. Flores:

For almost 10 years, I have pursued a satisfying career with the California Department of Environmental Management. At this point in my career, I would like to make a change to the private sector.

During my career, I have held positions as Environmental Project Manager, State Cleanup Section; Environmental Manager, Facilities Planning Section; and Environmental Scientist, Permits Section. My responsibilities have included managing the cleanup of hazardous waste sites, reviewing construction plans for water treatment facilities, and writing municipal permits. As a result, I have become adept at maneuvering through the bureaucracy to make things happen quickly.

I would welcome the opportunity to speak with you about my background and the potential areas where my expertise could be best utilized by your firm. A resume is enclosed detailing my qualifications.

Sincerely,

Patricia Butterfield

Peterson Engineering
354 Seventh Street
Houston, TX 77002

Dear Sir:

I am interested in applying for employment as a project
geologist in the Houston area. As you can see from my
resume, I have over 4 years of experience in managing
environmental assessments as well as designing groundwater
recovery and treatment systems.

I would like to meet with you to discuss my qualifications.
I believe that I would be a productive member of your
engineering staff.

Sincerely,

Bryan Pullman
43 Buffalo Bill Road
Omaha, NE 68129
(402) 555-5837

P.S. This is in response to your ad in Wednesday's *Star
Tribune* regarding the opening for a project geologist.

John K. Lai

Ms. Millicent Jones
Hancock Construction
1501 Pennsylvania Ave, NW
Washington, DC 20006

Dear Ms. Jones:

I am writing to follow up our telephone conversation on November 21st about Hancock Construction's need for a project manager in Beijing. As we discussed, I am currently winding up a construction project for Johnson, Inc. and am seeking a project management position overseas. My work experience combined with my fluency in Mandarin Chinese uniquely qualifies me for this position.

If I meet the requirements, I would be available for employment at the start of the new year. Relocation to Beijing presents no problems for my family.

I have enclosed my resume as you requested. I am looking forward to hearing from you soon.

Sincerely,

John K. Lai
20 West Concord Street
Dover, NH 03820
(603) 555-1703

9 DeSoto Drive
Baton Rouge, LA 70805

Southern Glassworks
350 Florida Street
New Orleans, LA 70112

To Whom It May Concern:

This letter is in response to the advertisement in the *New Orleans Picayune* on February 12, 1994 for an industrial engineer. Please accept my resume in consideration for this position.

With a master's degree in Industrial Engineering from Tulane University and seven years of work experience as an industrial engineer at Alexander Steel Company, I believe that I am well-suited to your firm's needs.

Thank you for your time. I look forward to hearing from you soon regarding the position at Southern Glassworks.

Sincerely,

Edgar Peters
(504) 555-1388

Enclosure

Charles Sanford

12 Mobile Drive, Birmingham, AL 35230

Ms. Alice Weaver
Southern Technologies
54 Perimeter Center
Atlanta, GA 30346

Dear Ms. Weaver:

During the past eight years, I have held engineering positions of increasing responsibility. As an experienced, creative, and results-oriented project engineer, I can provide your firm with the skills necessary to enhance productivity.

The following are a few of my accomplishments in my most recent position that may be of interest to your organization:

- Developed design improvements that resulted in over $5 million in production cost avoidance on current contracts.

- Conceived and coordinated the implementation of a Just-In-Time production control system which reduced associated WIP inventory levels.

- Lowered manufacturability cost of product designs by 25% and improved the operations productivity.

I have earned a bachelor's degree in Mechanical Engineering from Auburn University. I will receive my Master of Science in Business Administration from the University of Tennessee in June. My management coursework coupled with my expertise in evaluating product designs, analyzing production systems, and developing creative solutions, should enable me to make the kind of positive contributions your firm demands.

I have only presented a brief summary of my qualifications and accomplishments and therefore, would like to meet with you personally to further discuss how I could be an asset to Southern Technologies.

Sincerely,

Charles Sanford

Jack Olsen
P.O. Box 4680
Cambridge, MA 02139
(617) 555-4890

Riley Engineering
352 Congress Street
Portland, ME 04122

Dear Riley Engineering:

Currently, I am pursuing a Bachelor of Science degree in computer science at Massachusetts Institute of Technology. I plan to graduate on June 7, 1994.

Due to my prior work experience in information systems, the director of the Career Planning and Placement Office provided me with the profile of your firm.

I am extremely interested in obtaining a position at Riley Engineering. In particular, I would like an information systems or software development position that utilizes my computer programming language skills.

My resume has been enclosed for your review. Please do not hesitate to contact me if you need additional information.

I hope to hear from you soon.

Sincerely,

Jack Olsen

Enclosure

TOM HEALEY

606 WINSTON WAY • RALEIGH, NC • (919) 555-3218

New Technology Systems
2700 Main Street
Charlotte, NC 28255

To Whom It May Concern:

This letter is in response to the New Technology Systems's ad placed in the *Charlotte News* on January 19, 1994.

I have a master's degree in Business Administration and a Bachelor of Science in Mechanical Engineering. I am a registered professional engineer in the state of North Carolina as well as APICS certified in production and inventory management.

My work experience spans twenty-three years as a manufacturing engineer and production manager. Recent experiences have been in Just-In-Time and focused factories. I have demonstrated strengths in leading a manufacturing organization in support of an aggressive corporate strategy.

Enclosed is my resume detailing my work experience, certification, and educational background. I feel that my qualifications would be an asset to your firm.

I would welcome the opportunity for a personal interview to discuss the position at New Technology Systems.

Sincerely,

Tom Healey

Enclosure

Mr. George Hamil
International Steel
400 Hartz Avenue
Pittsburgh, PA 15222

Dear Mr. Hamil:

I am writing to inquire about any openings you may have for a process metallurgist in quality control. I have worked for 15 years with the United States Steel Corporation. During the past five years, my position has been that of Hot Mill Metallurgist responsible for all aspects of hot strip mill quality. I now desire to obtain a position with a small-sized steel manufacturer, such as your firm, with the opportunity for advancement into senior management.

My resume is enclosed for your review. If you should have an interest in further discussing my qualifications, please contact me at (219) 555-6457. Thank you for your time and consideration.

Sincerely,

Peter Dawson
420 Calumet Avenue
Gary, IN 46408

Enclosure

1038 Independence Drive
Dayton, OH 45469

Alex Hatcher
Quad Systems
3000 Sand Hill
Palo Alto, CA 94305

Dear Alex:

I have been extremely impressed by your firm's remarkable ability to be on the cutting edge of the marketplace's demand for new software engineering services. The progressive and innovative nature of Quad Systems appeals to me. These features are well-suited to my personality.

Presently, I am looking for a senior software engineer position, which provides responsibility for software projects from conceptual phase to finished product. Furthermore, I am looking to relocate in the Silicon Valley area.

A resume is enclosed that details my experience and qualifications. I look forward to meeting with you to explore the opportunities available at Quad Systems.

Please keep all contact personal and confidential.

Sincerely,

David Fortson
(513) 555-4429

Enclosure

VGM CAREER BOOKS

CAREER DIRECTORIES
Careers Encyclopedia
Dictionary of Occupational Titles
Occupational Outlook Handbook

CAREERS FOR
Animal Lovers
Bookworms
Computer Buffs
Crafty People
Culture Lovers
Environmental Types
Film Buffs
Foreign Language Aficionados
Good Samaritans
Gourmets
History Buffs
Kids at Heart
Nature Lovers
Number Crunchers
Sports Nuts
Travel Buffs

CAREERS IN
Accounting; Advertising; Business; Child Care; Communications; Computers; Education; Engineering; Finance; Government; Health Care; High Tech; Law; Marketing; Medicine; Science; Social & Rehabilitation Services

CAREER PLANNING
Beginning Entrepreneur
Career Planning & Development for College Students & Recent Graduates
Careers Checklists
Cover Letters They Don't Forget
Executive Job Search Strategies
Guide to Basic Resume Writing
Joyce Lain Kennedy's Career Book
Slam Dunk Resumes
Successful Interviewing for College Seniors

HOW TO
Approach an Advertising Agency and Walk Away with the Job You Want
Bounce Back Quickly After Losing Your Job
Change Your Career
Choose the Right Career
Get & Keep Your First Job
Get into the Right Law School
Get People to Do Things Your Way
Have a Winning Job Interview
Jump Start a Stalled Career
Land a Better Job
Launch Your Career in TV News
Make the Right Career Moves
Market Your College Degree
Move from College into a Secure Job
Negotiate the Raise You Deserve
Prepare a *Curriculum Vitae*
Prepare for College
Run Your Own Home Business
Succeed in College
Succeed in High School
Write Successful Cover Letters
Write a Winning Resume
Write Your College Application Essay

OPPORTUNITIES IN
Accounting
Acting
Advertising

Aerospace
Agriculture
Airline
Animal & Pet Care
Architecture
Automotive Service
Banking
Beauty Culture
Biological Sciences
Biotechnology
Book Publishing
Broadcasting
Building Construction Trades
Business Communication
Business Management
Cable Television
CAD/CAM
Carpentry
Chemistry
Child Care
Chiropractic
Civil Engineering
Cleaning Service
Commercial Art & Graphic Design
Computer Maintenance
Computer Science
Counseling & Development
Crafts
Culinary
Customer Service
Data Processing
Dental Care
Desktop Publishing
Direct Marketing
Drafting
Electrical Trades
Electronic & Electrical Engineering
Electronics
Energy
Engineering
Engineering Technology
Environmental
Eye Care
Fashion
Fast Food
Federal Government
Film
Financial
Fire Protection Services
Fitness
Food Services
Foreign Language
Forestry
Government Service
Health & Medical
High Tech
Home Economics
Homecare Services
Hospital Administration
Hotel & Motel Management
Human Resource Management
Information Systems
Installation & Repair
Insurance
Interior Design
International Business
Journalism
Laser Technology
Law
Law Enforcement & Criminal Justice
Library & Information Science
Machine Trades
Magazine Publishing
Marine & Maritime
Masonry
Marketing
Materials Science
Mechanical Engineering
Medical Imaging
Medical Technology

Metalworking
Military
Modeling
Music
Newspaper Publishing
Nonprofit Organizations
Nursing
Nutrition
Occupational Therapy
Office Occupations
Packaging Science
Paralegal
Paramedical
Part-time & Summer Jobs
Performing Arts
Petroleum
Pharmacy
Photography
Physical Therapy
Physician
Plastics
Plumbing & Pipe Fitting
Postal Service
Printing
Property Management
Psychology
Public Health
Public Relations
Purchasing
Real Estate
Recreation & Leisure
Refrigeration & Air Conditioning
Religious Service
Restaurant
Retailing
Robotics
Sales
Secretarial
Securities
Social Science
Social Work
Speech-Language Pathology
Sports & Athletics
Sports Medicine
State & Local Government
Teaching
Technical Writing & Communications
Telecommunications
Telemarketing
Television & Video
Theatrical Design & Production
Tool & Die
Transportation
Travel
Trucking
Veterinary Medicine
Visual Arts
Vocational & Technical
Warehousing
Waste Management
Welding
Word Processing
Writing
Your Own Service Business

RESUMES FOR
Advertising Careers
Banking and Financial Careers
College Students & Recent Graduates
Communications Careers
Education Careers
Engineering Careers
Environmental Careers
Health and Medical Careers
High School Graduates
High Tech Careers
Midcareer Job Changes
Sales and Marketing Careers
Scientific and Technical Careers

VGM Career Horizons
a division of *NTC Publishing Group*
4255 West Touhy Avenue
Lincolnwood, Illinois 60646 1975